PRIMARY PASTORAL CARE

Edited by
The Editorial Committee
The Journal of Pastoral Care

With a Foreword by
Bishop Leontine Turpeau Current Kelly

Journal of Pastoral Care Publications, Inc.
1990

PRIMARY PASTORAL CARE

Library of Congress Cataloging in Publication Data

Primary pastoral care / edited by the editorial committee, the Journal
    of pastoral care.
    p. cm.
    Articles originally published in the Journal of pastoral care,
    1985-1989.
    Includes index.
    Contents: Professional and ethical issues for ministers who
counsel / Mark C. Young -- A psychiatrist's view of transference and
countertransference in the pastoral relationship / Richard S.
Schwartz -- Referral as pastoral care / William B. Oglesby, Jr. --
Pastoral care of the mentally ill / Clark S. Aist -- Ritual in
pastoral care / Kenneth R. Mitchell -- Lay pastoral care / Ronald D.
Sunderland -- Pastoral care of the elderly / Melvin A. Kimble --
Pastoral care in the hospital / Frank S. Moyer.
    ISBN 0-929670-01-9 (acid-free)
    1. Pastoral theology. 2. Pastoral counseling. I. Journal of
pastoral care.
BV4016.P75 1990
253--dc20   90-40554
                                      CIP

Printed in the United States of America
on acid-free paper

Contents

Foreword

Primary Pastoral Care is an invaluable resource for the parish minister. The contributors to this significant compilation share vast experience, knowledge, and insight, and address with clarity and practicality many facets of the pastoral care field today. The historical, biblical, and theological rootage of healing ministry is inculcated with assurance of the import of clergy involvement. For despite modern technology and scientific advancement, there is no substitute for clergy as part of the helping ministry, particularly for members of faith communities.

In this fine volume, acknowledgement is made that clergy may be almost the last generalists; however, it is clear that clergy training, accessibility, and availability demand that clergypersons function with a high level of proficiency within a wide range of areas. Clarity, confidentiality, and competence are presented as rightful expectations of clientele who trust the minister's concern and wisdom in the helping process.

Professional and ethical issues are addressed in the sensitivity of modern society where litigation appears to be almost a common reflex. Pastors will appreciate the frank discussion of matters to consider before engaging in on-going therapy with a member of the congregation. It is of inestimable value, for example, to read a psychiatrist's focus on ways in which transference and countertransference may introduce stress and confusion into any pastoral relationship.

The common dilemma of when to refer a parishioner to insure that the most constructive help is given is treated so as not to violate the authenticity of the parish minister. It is evident that there is no need for pastors to feel alone or to jeopardize the health of parishoners when networking with other professionals and competencies is available.

With the movement to "deinstitutionalize" mental facilities pastors and congregations are faced with the responsibility of ministering to large numbers of persons who need particular care. The reality of the situation is vividly expressed in the words, "More and more the recovering mental patient is the person in front of us at the grocery check-out, or behind us at the movie theater, or across from us at McDonalds, or beside us at worship."

A congregational perspective of care of the mentally ill is shared in a step-by-step approach enabling pastors and people to minister to the deeply troubled in our communities. Guidance in the significance of rituals as a pastoral resource is an important companion essay at this point.

The involvement of lay people whose gifts lie in the area of the congregation's pastoral care ministry is exciting for those of us who see evangelism wholistically. Caring for the total person is more than "saving souls." With the overwhelming numbers of deeply troubled persons needing help, training persons in lay ministry is not only modeled after the pattern of Jesus and the disciples but understood, as one of the authors puts it, as "the act of ministering may be the mode in which the Gospel takes shape in their (lay persons) lives and those of others."

In retirement my firsthand knowledge of aging and ageism makes the chapter on "Pastoral Care for the Elderly" vivid and extremely satisfying. The fact that "pastors are obviously in a strategic position to respond to developmental needs and life-cycle crises of the aged and their families," combined with the realization that "everyone alive is aging," ensures a cheering section for pastors who perform this ministry well.

In the midst of writing this Foreword I was called to visit a dear friend who is confined in the intensive care unit of our local hospital. Modern technology is performing many of my friend's functions, even as basic one as breathing. Specialists are responding to differing bodily needs. The following words from the chapter "Pastoral Care in the Hospital" were fresh in my mind during my visit: "There are even greater challenges to pastoral care in the modern hospital of the late twentieth century!...patients, health care-givers, hospital administrators and society are engaged today in a highly technical and complex process within which roles, functions, and costs are carefully defined, monitored and contained."

The question is, "By what authority, then, does the minister go to the sick room?" When the nurse shared with my friend's wife and me the fact that their pastor had already been there we were comforted in ways that only the pastor's *call*, competency, and consent given by his members authenticates. The words of this patient's wife were sufficient affirmation of the text of *Primary Pastoral Care*. She said, "Bill is *completely* covered!"

The parish clergy's part in the caring process is that this sort of faith coverage, sought and understood by all believers, is what authenticates ministry. I thank God for the ways in which this book helps toward the realization of that reality.

— Leontine Turpeau Current Kelly
Retired Bishop
The United Methodist Church

Preface

In the Spring of 1985 at a meeting of what was then the Editorial Committee of *The Journal of Pastoral Care*, the members of that group got on the topic of the relationship between parish ministry and ministry in specialized settings. The discussion was lively and positive. So much so that it was decided to develop a series of short articles on particular pastoral care topics that would be of special interest to those parish pastors with deep interests in pastoral care and counseling.

It was the conviction of the editorial group at that meeting that specialists in the pastoral arts and sciences and ministers in parish settings do contribute to one another in sundry and depthful ways, but that these two groups of pastoral caregivers do not always have an adequate environment in which to share their experiences, theories, and understandings, including their respective literatures. Thus it was that a series of articles called "Primary Pastoral Care" came into being. These articles were published in *The Journal of Pastoral Care* between 1985 and 1989.

As it turned out, not all the topics originally identified resulted in articles. It was also discovered that a couple of pieces that came to *The Journal* quite spontaneously—over the transom, so to speak— seemed unusually relevant although not submitted as part of the Primary Pastoral Care Series. In the end—and indeed at some point the editors did need to call a halt to the series—a total of eight articles became a part of the series. And these pieces, along with this Preface and the Foreword by Bishop Leontine T. C. Kelly, now constitute *Primary Pastoral Care*.

We trust the original intention—to print "a good read" of practical articles which would acknowledge and demonstrate the essential concordance between pastoral care specialists and pastoral care generalists—is still intact.

> Orlo Strunk, Jr., *Chair*
> Sandra R. Brown
> John L. Florell
> William A. Miller
> Kenneth R. Mitchell
> John H. Patton

Professional and Ethical Issues for Ministers Who Counsel

MARK C. YOUNG, M.DIV., M.S.

Co-pastor, Ebenezer United Methodist Church,
2564 Hess Road, Fallston, MD 21047

P arish clergy are often the first professional people that members of a congregation seek out for help. This is true for a variety of reasons, but especially because of their easy accessibility and availability. Indeed, in many cases a comfortable acquaintance already exists between the minister and parishioner. The help needed may vary from a specific situation requiring little expertise to an emotional issue involving actual psychopathology. Consequently, the parish minister must function with a high level of proficiency in a wide range of areas. In a professional world involving evermore-narrow fields of specialization, clergy are among the last generalists.

While this provides wonderful opportunities for clergy to assist people, we must recognize that the necessary knowledge or skill to manage any and every situation are not bestowed upon ministers by seminary training, ordination or religious vows. This is especially true of circumstances with parishioners involving significant pathology or requiring long-term counseling. Such situations should be left to those persons who have received clinical training as specialized pastoral counselors, psychologists, psychiatrists, and the like.

This general rule is easily defended on very practical grounds. Most clergy do not possess the in-depth training and skill required to handle such issues as diagnosis, transference, resistance, or the psychodynamic interpretation of behavior, all of which are very important aspects of ongoing therapy. Further, few parish ministers can devote sufficient time on a regular basis to engage a number of individuals, couples, or families in extended counseling. The reality of role blending is another difficult factor to manage, and the public "fish bowl" effect of many parish settings makes privacy and confidentiality difficult to ensure. Finally, those serving in parishes need to be sensitive to the litigious nature of our society and the ever-increasing possibility of malpractice suits.

While this may be a plausible general rule, the reality remains that many clergy are involved in providing long-term therapy to persons in need, often for equally understandable reasons. A minister serving in a rural parish, for example, may be the only person available with any training at all. Many people do not trust secular psychologists or psychiatrists and will not seek help from them even when referred by their pastor. We do not live in a perfect world or under ideal conditions where general rules always apply. Thus, for many people, pastoral therapy is a reality and is defined simply as the counseling that they receive from their minister regardless of his or her training.

This being the case, there are a number of professional and ethical issues that parish clergy and vowed religious should consider before engaging in ongoing therapy with a member of the congregation. These considerations may be grouped under the headings of clarity, confidentiality, and competence.

Clarity

When engaging in ongoing therapy with a parishioner, the minister must first of all recognize the existence of dual roles inherent in the relationship. From the perspective of the parishioner, the minister is functioning as both a pastor and a therapist, and while this initially seems quite obvious, it must always be kept in mind. Both roles involve issues of trust, power, and dependency, and thus inculcate vulnerability in the client. When the roles are combined in the person of one minister, the client's vulnerability is magnified. The blending of the relational roles increases the potential for abuse and exploitation, however unintentional these might be. Therefore special care must be taken to ensure the welfare of the client. To do this, the pastoral counselor must work to establish clarity in a number of areas.

To begin, the counselors must be clear in their own minds about their ability to deal with the presenting problems. We all have limitations and individuals engaging in therapy must be honest with themselves and their clients about these limits. Ministers must be willing to discuss in an open and direct manner their abilities and skill levels in dealing with specific situations. While apparently threatening to raise doubt and lower client confidence in a pastor, this openness actually has the opposite effect. Such clarity increases the level of trust within the relationship and allows the client to raise issues of expectation for the therapy as well.

Secondly, the pastoral counselor should work to clearly establish the parameters of the counseling relationship. A therapeutic alliance with a given parishioner is different from an ongoing relationship involving typical pastoral care which takes place in a variety of settings during assorted times of varying lengths. The minister offers care during home and hospital visits, in discussions surrounding worship and program meetings, over the telephone, and in casual conversations. In many cases, clergy will take the initiative to seek out opportunities to address pastoral care issues.

Therapy, on the other hand, should take place within a closed office at regular and specified times. The duration of the sessions should be established and limited. Typically sessions range between forty-five and sixty minutes. The minister should be clear that therapeutic issues will be dealt with only during the counseling sessions and must avoid additional discussion in other settings. The client is responsible for coming to the minister's office and keeping the appointments. Policies dealing with cancellations, emergency needs, and telephone calls should be delineated and discussed.

To further separate the roles of pastor and therapist, a fee for service might be charged for the counseling. Ongoing therapy provides individual parishioners with a disproportionate amount of pastoral time and is perhaps above and beyond the normal duties of the minister. Pastors are within their rights to expect reasonable remuneration for this service. (This of course should be discussed and cleared through the governing body of the church. Raising such issues affords the minister an excellent opportunity to establish clarity with the congregational representatives concerning pastoral duties and expectations.) This becomes a viable means for clergy and vowed religious to care for themselves and set limits.

Open and direct discussion of fees can prove fruitful on a therapeutic level. For clients, fees are often a significant therapeutic concern involving self-esteem, motivation, and commitment. Regardless of this value, the minister is obliged to establish clarity concerning the amount of the fee, the method of payment, and any policy concerning collection of delinquent monies. These are often difficult issues for religious professionals, which suggests the need for ministers to think these issues through clearly for themselves.

Another area of discussion concerning the parameters of the counseling relationship involves the delineation of the client's rights and the therapist's responsibilities. Clients have the right to competent care, which is in turn the responsibility of the therapist. Such care is characterized by the full and active participation of the client in a discussion of reasonable expectations and the setting of therapeutic goals. Clients have the right to understand the therapeutic techniques and procedures which will be employed, and the counselor has a responsibility to elaborate on these to the satisfaction of the client. Additionally, the client has the right of confidentiality and the need to know the limits of confidential communication.

Finally, clients should be informed of the potential risks involved in counseling. There are potential dangers whenever one enters a relationship involving the intensity often experienced in therapy. Clients may discover things about themselves or their past that they would rather not know. They may change in significant ways and relate differently to their significant others. Their condition may seem to grow worse before improving. The possibilities are numerous, and the wise counselor will raise such concerns with the client.

Overall, clarity concerning the therapeutic relationship is an important and crucial issue because it ensures the client's welfare. The pastoral counselor has a responsibility to obtain informed consent from the client to engage in therapy. This means that individuals must be presented with information concerning the therapeutic process sufficient to enable them to make responsible decisions regarding the intended therapy. When this is done well, the counseling relationship will be established on firm foundations. Clarity is an empowering force that reduces the risks inherent in the vulnerability of the therapeutic relationship.

Confidentiality

The matter of confidentiality is basic to all forms of counseling. In fact, it is a crucial issue in nearly all types of helping relationships. As mentioned previously, confidentiality is a fundamental right of the client and a significant responsibility of the therapist. It is therefore important to establish the meaning and boundaries of confidentiality.

Essentially, the prerogative of confidentiality arises out of the basic constitutional right to privacy enjoyed by members of our society. Privacy is the power that individuals possess to determine for themselves what, if any, personal information will be shared with others. It involves exercising the freedom of self-determination and guards the dignity of each human person. When a client enters a therapeutic relationship with a minister, that individual chooses to yield some degree of personal privacy by sharing intimate information with another. Doing so is an act of meaningful trust that must not be abused.

Confidentiality is the professional standard of conduct that obliges the minister, or any counselor, to maintain this sacred trust. The minister promises to preserve the client's privacy by refusing to share the information with others. Everything that is revealed by the client in therapy is held in confidence by the counselor. This has serious implications for ministers who counsel with their own parishioners.

Because parishes are often closely knit communities, the minister must exercise caution when interacting within the congregation. The client may or may not be open with others about the counseling, and the minister must take care to protect the client's choice in this matter. Out of concern, friends and members of the family who are aware of the therapeutic affiliation may ask the minister how the individual is doing. The minister must be clear when responding that such information can not be shared. Even such seemingly innocuous statements as "she's really struggling right now" or "he's doing much better" are ethically forbidden. Such statements would violate the privacy of the client.

There are, however, limits to confidentiality, and circumstances under which the minister may breach confidence. These should be spelled out for the client. Basically there are two types of circumstances under which the religious professional is freed from the obligation of this fundamental responsibility.

The first circumstance involves situations where the clients themselves grant this freedom. This is especially important with respect to consultation with other professionals. In these instances the minister is wise to have the client sign a consent form. As another example, a client might desire the pastor to speak with a family member about a particular issue within the counseling. In these cases, the minister should exercise caution and gain specificity from the client by thoroughly discussing the possible consequences in session before carrying out the request.

The second circumstance limiting confidentiality concerns situations of public peril. The principle involved here is that individual privacy and private communication cease when public peril begins. Within the counseling setting, public peril refers to situations involving child abuse, homicide, or suicide. If clients reveal to the minister that they have abused or intend to abuse a minor child, the minister is obligated by law to report this to the appropriate governmental child protective service for investigation. Similarly, if clients reveal that they have committed murder or intend homicide, the minister is obligated to report this information to the appropriate authorities and to warn any potential victims. When suicidal ideations emerge within the counseling, the therapist must determine whether the clients intend to harm themselves and possess the means to do so. If suicide is found to be a real risk, again the minister must take appropriate action to prevent it.

In all of these situations of public peril, a considerable burden falls upon the counselor to exercise sound judgment. While confidentiality is broken, the therapist is still responsible for maintaining client welfare. Thus, the minister must proceed in a manner that both ensures public safety and is sensitive to the needs and feelings of the client. This is not an easy balance to attain. Those who counsel would be well advised to think these situations through in advance of their actual occurrence. Clients have the right and need to know at the beginning of therapy that these limits to confidentiality exist.

Finally, a word is necessary concerning the concept of privileged communication and its association with confidentiality. This is a legal concept whereby information that is gained in a relationship involving privileged communication is precluded from disclosure in court or other legal proceedings. The laws of the various states spell out which relationships are specifically granted privilege. These usually include attorney/client, physician/patient, husband/wife, and priest/penitent relationships. Some states grant privilege to licensed psychologist/ client affiliations.

Ministers should be clear that their counseling relationships are not covered by the concept of privileged communication. Therapy does not constitute a confessional or penitential situation, nor are most ministers licensed to practice psychology. Thus, ministers must be aware that they can be subpoenaed into court for testimony. In such situations, they would still need to gain the client's permission to share information lest they breach confidentiality. If the client will not grant such permission, the counselor will be in a difficult ethical dilemma. Because we live in a highly litigious society, clergy are ever more vulnerable to such possibilities.

Competence

As previously noted, an overarching ethical principle that structures the therapeutic relationship between any counselor and client is the need to ensure client welfare. Parishioners who engage in counseling with their ministers have the right to expect and receive competent care. Yet the concept of competence is difficult to define. It involves more than having received specific training, possessing the correct academic degrees, or knowing a variety of techniques. These certainly contribute to competence, but they do not guarantee it.

Rather, competent care also encompasses the professional's ability to enter into and maintain intimate relationships with warmth, empathy, and unconditional acceptance. It involves understanding one's own motivations and maintaining watchfulness over them to protect the integrity of the therapeutic alliance. It encompasses the minister's sense of ethical responsibility and professional code of conduct as well.

Competence further includes the professional person's awareness of respective personal strengths and abilities as well as limitations and deficiencies. It involves the healthy and responsible acknowledgement of the boundaries of one's therapeutic capabilities. No one person can master all of the knowledge associated with the complex thoughts, feelings, and behaviors of human beings. Our experience and expertise are necessarily limited, and the competent professional is one who can freely admit this. Once again, those ministering to others through counseling must be clear about themselves.

Perhaps two helpful questions ministers can ask in counseling situations are: "Do I truly understand the problem that is being presented?" and "Do I possess the knowledge, experience, and training necessary to adequately meet the needs of this situation?" Answering these questions will provide the therapist with a sense of personal competence and help to direct individual energies. Affirmative responses will empower greater confidence and enable the minister to proceed. Negative responses require the minister to hesitate, but do not necessarily preclude the minister's participation in helping the parishioner. Rather, they require the exploration of several options.

Powerfully negative responses to these questions indicate that the minister does need to refer the parishioner to another professional in the mental health field, where possible. There should be no shame associated with this as referral is a positive way to help many people. Clergy can remain a potent force in the helping process by taking a supportive role. Another option is to seek consultation with a person more experienced in psychotherapeutic endeavors. Such consultation may serve to elucidate the problem and equip the minister to proceed.

Both referral and consultation raise the need for clergy to establish a network of affiliations with other helping professionals. Ideally, those who responsibly engage in counseling will establish and maintain relationships with a psychiatrist or psychologist, a physician, and an attorney. They would be wise to familiarize themselves with the local social services departments, law enforcement agencies, procedures of area hospitals, detoxification facilities, Alcoholic Anonymous and Al-Anon groups, urologists, and gynecologists, as well as the emergency procedure of their area hospitals. Such knowledge and familiarity will prove quite useful to the overall ministry.

Another option for the minister who is unsure in a counseling situation entails the pursuit of further training and supervision. Clergy who offer a significant amount of counseling should give this option serious consideration. Supervision especially is a significant way to increase one's clinical skill and safeguard an ongoing therapeutic responsibility. It provides the minister with a collaborative environment to explore both client and counselor issues.

In summary, ministers who engage in counseling with parishioners are responsible for providing competent care. The client is entitled to such, and client welfare is an essential requirement in the process. While competence is difficult to define, it remains the minister's duty to establish it. When this is not possible, the counselor should refer the person to another helping professional. Those engaging in a significant amount of ongoing therapy are encouraged to seek specific training and supervision.

A Psychiatrist's View of Transference and Countertransference in the Pastoral Relationship

RICHARD S. SCHWARTZ, M.D.,

Associate Director, Adult Outpatient Clinic,
McLean Hospital,
115 Mill Street, Belmont, MA 02178

There is a certain presumptuousness to a psychiatrist offering his thoughts about transference and countertransference in the pastoral relationship. As a psychiatrist, I have done my share of thinking about these phenomena, but since I do not work within a pastoral relationship myself, I obviously must discuss their effects on that specific relationship without first-hand experience. Since that fact may raise questions about my intentions, I will first explain the origin of this essay.

I was asked to speak on this subject as part of a symposium on stress in the pastoral relationship. The request came from a rabbi. After I accepted his invitation, I wondered why I had been willing to discuss a topic that is outside my own experience. I soon realized that the answer took me to the very heart of the topic. At least in part, I began this essay because of my own transference to a pastoral figure. Simply put, a rabbi called, told me what he wanted me to do, and I did it. My sense of power and authority behind his request was based not on the intention or the personal attributes of the particular individual involved, but on other figures out of my past. In other words, my response was based on transference, and more narrowly, transference elicited from me by someone's pastoral role.

The Nature of Transference

Transference was "discovered" by Freud when he realized that a patient was reacting to him, not as he was, but as if he were another version of her father.[1] Just as important was his realization that the patient was unaware of this aspect of her response to him. From

---

[1] Sigmund Freud, "Fragment of an Analysis of a Case of Hysteria," in *Complete Psychological Works*, V(II. 7 (London: Hogarth, 1953), pp. 7-122.

these beginnings there developed a definition of transference as "a distorted and inappropriate response derived from unresolved unconscious conflicts in (a person's) past."[2]

It is actually a simple concept. It just says that we are not capable of entering into a new relationship as something genuinely and completely new. Instead, our experience of people in the present is colored by how we have experienced important figures in our past. The more problematic past relationships have been and the less successful we have been in seeing them clearly, the more likely they are to color our present responses in ways of which we are unaware.

Harry Stack Sullivan invented a term, "parataxic distortion," that he preferred to transference.[3] The term never entered general usage, but the notion behind the term has. Transference tended to be used to describe something that occurred in a psychotherapeutic relationship. The point that Sullivan was trying to make with his neologism is that these distortions are an aspect of all human interactions, that they are part of the way in which we are all constantly dealing with one another, including, of course, in the pastoral relationship.

The concept of countertransference is a little more confusing because it is actually used in three different ways. In reading papers that refer to countertransference, it is important to decide which definition the author is using. The narrowest definition of countertransference is transference in the therapist; that is, a distorted and inappropriate response derived from unconscious conflicts in the therapist's past. A second important use of the word countertransference is to describe the responses in the therapist evoked by the patient's transference to him or her; that is to say, your own response to the ways in which a patient insists on mis-perceiving you. The last use of the word is, I think, too general to be useful, but may still be encountered. It is countertransference as all the therapist's emotional responses to the patient.

---

[2]Ralph R. Greenson, "Loving, Hating and Indifference Toward the Patient," in *Exploration in Psychoanalysis* (New York, NY: International Universities Press, 1978), p. 507.

[3]Harry Stack Sullivan, *Conceptions of Modern Psychiatry* (New York, NY: Norton, 1940), p. 92.

Having laid out these definitions, let me now turn to two questions: First, what is the connection between countertransference and stress? Second, what types of transference and countertransference might be particularly characteristic of the pastoral relationship?

The Stress of Transference and Countertransference

The question of stress can be approached through each of the first two definitions of countertransference. First, if we are having distorted and inappropriate responses to a client derived from unresolved conflicts in our past, one of two things can happen. If we are completely unaware that this is going on, we may be very successful in avoiding stress, but we risk doing immeasurable harm to the client whom we are treating as different from what he or she really is. If we are aware of something distorting our responses, then we face the stress of needing continuously to monitor and do battle with powerful forces within ourselves; and if the battle goes on too long or requires too much energy, we not only feel drained by the effort, but once again we risk missing who the client actually is due to the need to focus attention on ourselves. In either case, there are two ways to avoid doing harm. We can either stop working with the type of person who stirs up a particular conflict within us or we can seek therapy ourselves in order better to separate out the past from the present.

The second definition of countertransference, the therapist's response to the patient's transference, also locates another major source of stress in helping relationships. Most simply put, to be loved, to be hated, to be worshipped, to be despised evokes powerful feelings even in the healthiest of us. It is very stressful to bear these feelings without *doing* something about them, whether it is to counter-attack in the face of being hated, to accept the rewards of being loved, or simply to place distance between ourselves and someone we could otherwise help in order to moderate the feelings. It is the great difficulty and stress of not allowing ourselves the ordinary reciprocal response to a powerful feeling that led Freud to speak of "working with highly explosive forces" in a discussion of transference love.[4]

---

[4]Sigmund Freud, "Observations on Transference–Love," in *Complete Psychological Works*, Vol. 12 (London: Hogarth, 1953), p. 170.

But there is another aspect to this stress. The nature of transference is that it actively negates who you are. It takes away your identity and replaces it with another. I once had a patient who came in day after day and described her experience of me as a cruel rigid doctor who sought out only what was hateful in her. Faced with this image of me over time, it was hard not to hate in return or give in to despair. Working with this patient in that phase of her treatment was one of the most exhausting experiences I have had as a psychiatrist. Another woman saw me quite differently. She returned from a religious retreat and, with some embarrassment, reported that, in an exercise where they were asked to visualize a representation of God, she found herself seeing me. Again, there is a stressful temptation. In this case the danger is to be seduced into thinking that this woman was remarkably perceptive in her views.

Specific Transference in Pastoral Relationships

The example of a therapist coming to embody a patient's image of God moves us to consider more directly the pastoral relationship. Let me introduce one more concept—"preformed transference." Most transference emerges gradually over the course of an intensely intimate relationship. Sometimes, however, a person seems to greet you in the very first encounter as though you are someone other than who you are and, before you even have a chance to see it coming, something is awry. It is as though their transference to you was prepared in advance of your arrival and all you had to do was step into the role. In fact, I think these preformed transferences are essentially transferences to somebody's role, to the position that you occupy. The nature of these preformed transferences therefore differs from role to role. The one's most often encountered by religious figures differ from those I most often encounter as a physician. I will however suggest some preformed transferences that I suspect figure importantly in many pastoral relationships. In each of these transferences, there will be a mixture of three elements. First, the usual aspects of past family relationships; second, transference based on previous pastoral relationships; and third, transference based on a person's experience of his or her relationship to God. (For a thoughtful debate on whether the resolution of transference is an appropriate goal in pastoral care, I recommend two opposing papers by Ahlskog[5] and Schlauch.[6] I will limit myself to considering its impact on the relationship.)

The example of my response to the rabbi who invited me to consider this topic was a preformed transference to a pastoral figure as an authority. My transference to the role extended to his person and finally to his words, although I am sure that he did not experience himself as bringing any authority to bear on me. This "religious authority transference" has two faces. It can lead to more respect than you perhaps deserve or, if someone's experience with religious authority has been less benign, it can lead to unexpected hatred and suspicion, as with a Catholic patient of mine who believed people become nuns and priests in order to use authority to crush others.

Another set of preformed transferences might center around a pastoral figure as a source of forgiveness and redemption. The patient I mentioned earlier who saw me as drawing forth only hateful things from her was at the same time in love with a priest, who loved her in return. She hoped that, because of their love, she might be able to stop experiencing herself as filled with anger and hate. While some of the hope was based in their actual love, some of it was also a transference hope that depended on her lover having been a priest.

A final transference category involves the need for clergy to be more than human. A colleague told me of a rabbi who served his congregation well in his formal duties but tended to be preoccupied in places like the supermarket, where he would never recognize or say hello to people he met. As his congregation got angrier, he tried to explain to them, "Rabbi's are only human beings." Essentially, he was saying, "Look, this wish that I be perfect is transference and you have got to deal with who I really am instead of transference." His response was true, perhaps even wise, but, in the face of his congregation's transference needs, it missed the mark. He was asked to leave. That is the power of transference .

---

[5]Gary R. Ahlskog, "The Paradox of Pastoral Psychotherapy," *The Journal of Pastoral Care*, 1987, Vol. 41, No. 4, pp. 311-318.

[6]Chris R. Schlauch, "Defining Pastoral Psychotherapy II," *The Journal of Pastoral Care*, 1987, Vol. 41, No. 4, pp. 319-327.

Sexual Dangers

There is one other aspect of the power of transference and countertransference that requires specific mention. It is the exploitation of transference and the indulgence of countertransference that occurs in sexual relations between a therapist and client. Because of my own idealizing transference to clergy, I would like to think that the subject is irrelevant to pastoral relationships, but unfortunately we know that it is not. Like all sexual exploitation, sexual relations between therapist and client is an abuse of power, but the specific power that it abuses is the power of transference. It is primarily because of transference distortions and idealizations that the client is unable simply to say, "This will not be helpful to me," and to walk out. Similarly, since I think that relatively few true sociopaths become either therapists or clergy, countertransference must play a role as well. The nature of the countertransference may be more complicated than it might first seem, however.

Certainly, there is countertransference-based expression of sexual impulses that belong elsewhere. But there must also be major countertransference problems in the area of the therapist's narcissism; that is to say, in the regulation of self-esteem. Both newspaper articles and more scholarly surveys suggest that therapists who have sex with patients feel that they do so in the best interest of the patient, to provide her (and it is usually a "her") with a critical experience essential to her development, of which she would otherwise be deprived. Of course, this is a self-serving rationalization, but I think it also accurately reflects the therapist's grandiose notion about the specialness of the gift that he can give to his patient, a view that the patient, for reasons of her own transference, supports. Without narcissistic self-deception, the sexual impulses would be much more easily controlled.

A unique aspect of your position as clergy, however the specifics may be understood in your various faiths, is your relationship with God. The specialness of that relationship most often engenders a sense of humility, but it can also become the basis for an exaggerated sense of what you can offer others through your person rather than your role. In pastoral counseling, this sense of personal specialness represents a specific countertransference danger to those that you counsel because their own transferences to you make them very vulnerable.

Several years ago, a committee of the American Psychiatric Association investigated allegations of psychiatrist-patient sex. They found a consistently repeated series of steps leading up to sex between psychiatrist and patient. The steps were:

1. Calling the patient by the first name.
2. Extending the duration of sessions.
3. Rearranging appointment times outside of working hours, at the patient's request.
4. Giving personal information about oneself to the patient.
5. Hugging.
6. Fondling.
7. Intercourse.[7]

(Of course, Step 1 does not invariably lead to Step 7, but it is very hard to get to Step 7 without beginning with Step 1.) In related work, the committee investigated whatever specific therapies carried more risk of patient sexual abuse than others and, if so, what characteristics they shared. They found two: a first name basis between doctor and patient and flexible appointments without defined length or frequency.[8] Both of these characteristics are often present in pastoral counseling. Should this be a reason for concern? I am not sure. To apply a study of doctors to clergy is not scientifically sound. Moreover, religious beliefs and religious sanctions are potent forces. On the other hand, I once thought that the Hippocratic Oath was a more potent force than it appears to be, so perhaps these cautions are not misplaced.

Conclusion

In my discussion I have tried to focus on the ways in which transference and countertransference may introduce stress and confusion into any pastoral relationship. Their importance is not limited to pastoral counseling where, as in psychotherapy, they can also be used as tools for understanding an individual's past. Past experiences can always distort our perception of the present, but the danger from these distortions is particularly great when there is a power

---

[7]Nanette Gartrell, Judith Herman, *et al.*, "Psychiatrist-Patient Sexual Contact: Results of a National Survey, 1: Prevalence," *American Journal of Psychiatry*, 1986, Vol. 143, No. 9.

[8]Shervert Frazier, personal communication, 1987.

gradient in the relationship, as is inevitably created when one person asks another for help.

These dangers can be minimized by combining three approaches which are usually part of pastoral counseling programs but tend to be absent from the everyday life of most clergy. The first is education about these phenomena, the approach that I have taken in this paper. The second is to seek knowledge of one's own characteristic distortions through introspection or therapy. The third is to open one's work to the view of supportive peers and supervisors, who, more removed from these powerful forces, may better be able to detect their presence. But the task is never easy.

Referral as Pastoral Care

WILLIAM B. OGLESBY, JR, Ph.D.*
6518 Ivanhoe Dr.
Mechanicsville, VA 23111

"There is a loneliness in the ministry. It is the kind of loneliness that is shared by everyone in professional life who daily is confronted with issues and problems for which there is no 'blueprint.' It is a loneliness which wells up whenever decisions must be made that affect the lives of others, and for which there can be no definite assurance as to the final outcome. It is a loneliness which becomes increasingly poignant for ministers who realize that they deal with time and eternity—that the questions posed have to do with life and death and life again. It is a loneliness which tends to overwhelm when it emerges in a realistic consciousness of personal inadequacy."[1]

I wrote those words almost exactly twenty years ago. We were in the struggle and turmoil of the 1960's. In retrospect I now relive those painful times; and in the process become aware of how little we knew of that which was yet to come—Watergate, world terrorism, nuclear disaster, agony in drug and substance abuse, the list runs on. And now, just over a decade from the Twenty-First Century, it is a mercy that we cannot foresee tomorrow, else we would be completely overwhelmed. And ancient words, "Sufficient unto the day is the evil thereof," [2] bring comfort that we do not need to relive yesterday and have no way of fending off tomorrow, although, properly, we learn from the former and plan for the latter as best we can.

Many will remember the opening paragraph cited above as the introductory words of my book on referral. The book moved through several printings by three publishers, although presently it is

---

*The author is Professor Emeritus of Pastoral Counseling, Union Theological Seminary in Virginia, Richmond, Virginia.

[1]William B. Oglesby, Jr., *Referral in Pastoral Counseling* (Englewood Cliffs, NJ: Prentice Hall, Inc., 1968). (Later published by Fortress Press and Abingdon Press, 1978), p. 15.

[2]Matthew 5:34, KJV.

out of print. In all likelihood I shall not revise it; its substance is, I believe, still sound but for it to be reprinted would require an update, which is not at the top of my priority list just now. So it is that I welcome the invitation from *The Journal* editors that I prepare this essay. Indeed, the piece might well be titled "Referral Revisited."

A case can be made for the fact that much of the professional loneliness in ministry in the mid-60's was in some sense self-imposed. We had gone from the seminaries in a kind of professional isolation marked by a hesitance to trust fellow clergy with our practice of ministry, however defined. Few submitted sermons to colleagues for critique either before or after delivery; even fewer brought verbatim reconstructions of pastoral conversations as a means for enhancing care delivery. Moreover, there was a kind of "mystique" held by the clergy in their perception of professional personnel in the helping enterprises. The physician, the psychiatrist, the clinical psychologist, the psychiatric social worker and others were often perceived as a "breed apart" who had data and experience not possessed by the parish minister. As a consequence, many felt a kind of awe marked by uncertainty when a parishioner was referred to such a person. Did the referral signify failure on the part of the minister? Did refusal to refer signify an imperialism on the part of the minister? Would referral interrupt, if not destroy, the pastoral relationship with the parishioner? These are only a few of the complex factors involved in professional colleagueship in many instances twenty years ago.

I am pleased to discover that much progress has been made, as evidenced in the situation of the mid-1980's. One of the crucial factors in this progress is the occurrence of professional consultation by the clergy in discovering the most effective means for dealing with the human situation. Increasingly it is possible to discern the extent to which the resources of the ministry are recognized and welcomed by the helping professions. Paul Pruyser's *The Minister as Diagnostician*[3] appeals to clergy to bring their own discipline to bear on the human situation and notes that it is not helpful when ministers speak only as psychologists or social workers. He expects that clergy will have a basic awareness of the advances that have been made in the behavioral sciences but notes that the true contribution of the clergy is the representation of the heritage of faith in the reso-

---

[3]Paul W. Pruyser, *The Minister as Diagnostician* (Philadelphia, PA: The Westminster Press, 1976).

lution of human distress. Increasingly, clergy have become a part of the "healing team" in hospitals, mental health centers, psychiatric treatment institutions and their input valued as a significant factor in human restoration.

This transition in the past two decades has done much to break down the tacit but powerful barrier between the sciences and theology which emerged in the days of the Awakening. No longer is it necessary to see "truth" as emerging only through empirical investigation on the one hand or through revelation on the other. More and more we are aware of the fact that all truth is of God and that in wrestling with the data of investigative process we are, as the ancient saying goes, "thinking His thoughts after Him."

Even so, it is possible to paint too rosy a picture as we move toward the end of the Twentieth Century. Much progress has been made, and much remains to be done. Thus, the purpose of this essay is to take courage from the past and move toward the future.

A Network of Human Assistance

It is well from time to time for all of us in ministry to review the scope of our allies in meeting human need. The usual, although not necessarily the primary, starting point is the considerable presence of the secular helping professions. Every urban area has scores of persons and institutions which are dedicated to the relief of human suffering. These resources run the gamut of highly skilled personnel in medicine, psychiatry, guidance, counseling, nursing, substance abuse, psychology, social work, and the list runs on. Most urban areas coordinate these services through some sort of community council or human need resources organization and listings of available personnel and programs are readily accessible to clergy. But having this knowledge is only a first step in the process of pastoral care as referral. It is crucial that ministers become familiar with the exact nature of the resources and have more than a passing acquaintance with the persons who provide the services.

Alongside these professional personnel there is a widespread network of volunteer persons who are committed to the alleviation of suffering and the providing of support in all manner of human struggle. Ordinarily these people are identified with a particular human situation for which they have a personal investment. Perhaps the most widely known of these is Alcoholics Anonymous together with the cognate services such as Alanon, Alateen and the like. The basic idea of AA has carried over into a plethora of groups dealing with some particular human distress such as Gamblers Anonymous, Overeaters Anonymous, and the like. The primary principle in such confederations is that those who have experienced the distress and are in the process of recovery are in an excellent position to be of help to persons still enmeshed in the addiction.

A variation on this theme is the presence of groups that deal primarily with terminal disease. Many communities have a "Make Today Count" program which is designed to enable persons "to live as long as they are alive." More regionally oriented groups of the same genre are "Can-surmount" designed to support persons and their families in dealing with cancer, and similar support groups for other identifiable physical ailments. From the same perspective but with a different structure the Hospice Movement has provided support both for terminal patients and their families. I do not know of any widespread "directory" of these types of helping groups, but investigation through community agencies is ordinarily the best way to discover what is available in one's own area.

Alongside these community resources there is the often overlooked support of the People of God. Many faith groups maintain human services organizations in urban areas which include but are not limited to such things as foster care, adoption, family and marriage counseling, mental retardation, problems of aging, and the like. Pastoral Counseling Centers provide expert care delivery in increasing numbers. In like fashion, particular congregations can identify persons within their membership who have special interests and skills to function in care delivery. We are moving beyond the time when it was expected that the clergy undertake the primary if not sole responsibility for care delivery. More and more we realize that ministry is the gift of God to the people of God and not solely to the clergy. Programs have been developed to assist congregations fulfill their role as burden bearers, and books such as *The Tender Shepherd*[4] by John Killinger document what can be done in a local congregation.

---

[4]John Killinger, *The Tender Shepherd* (Nashville, TN: Abingdon Press, 1985).

When to Refer

In light of this considerable array of resources available to the parish minister there still remains the issue of when he or she can be certain—or as certain as is humanly possible—of when direct utilization is to be made. Twenty years ago I noted that the dilemma turned on the clergy's uncertainty regarding the criteria for continuing to attempt to provide direct services or to enlist assistance from someone else in working for the welfare of the parishioner. It is not a simple issue, nor has the passage of the two decades provided an easy answer. Ordinarily, the tension emerges in the clergy being too quick to refer on the one hand or too slow to refer on the other. Who among us has not felt this dilemma and who among us can claim to have arrived at a "fail-safe" solution?

These two obvious negative responses to human suffering, *i.e.,* for the minister to be "too quick" to refer or "too slow" to refer merit attention. In many instances, of course, these are not genuine options. Confronted with certain types of personal need, such as a sudden coronary while speaking with the pastor in the study, poses no question whatsoever. The list of these crisis-type experiences is so obvious that there is no need for elaboration. Clearly there is no way that the minister's process of referral can come "too quickly" in getting the parishioner in touch with appropriate emergency resources. In like manner, and taken from almost the same list, any responsible minister will certainly not delay to enlist professional assistance for the person.

But when we move beyond these readily apparent situations the issue becomes cloudy. Many a minister has referred a parishioner when he or she could lay hold on personal resources which would prove of value in moving toward some sort of resolution. This does not mean that referral would be postponed indefinitely. But if the situation was not one of acute crisis or if it appeared in some sense to be chronic, then the minister may be in a position to work with the parishioner in wrestling with the resistances which often are involved in moving toward resolution. The question Jesus addressed to the paralytic as recorded in John 6 may be relevant at such a juncture.

"Do you want to be healed?"[5] It is not a matter to be taken lightly. To be sure the Gospel account is not presented as a "verbatim" question in line with our own reproduction of pastoral conversations. Thus, there is no obvious reason why any one of us would ask the question in its narrative form. But the meaning behind the question is quite relevant. Who among us does not continue in some sort of health-destroying process or attitude, deploring it the while, and yet unwilling to move toward its elimination? "Do you really want to get well?" The fact is that part of us *does* want healing, but a part of us *does not.* I have never known a person who wanted to be an alcoholic but I have known personally hundreds of alcoholics. "Do you want to be healed?" The usual internal—unstated—answer is, "Well, yes I do; but I am sure I can work it out. " The arresting title of Vernon Johnson's book *I'll Quit Tomorrow*[6] is paradigmatic. It certainly applies to alcoholics; but it also applies to all of us who are aware of those things that disturb us, but who resist doing anything about them. All of this is not to say that the minister is the only one who can deal with such resistances; it does mean that those of us in ministry have primary access to people in a fashion not granted to our colleagues in the helping professions. Moreover, our professional work is set in the context of those values which transcend but do not ignore physical and emotional distresses. For whatever reason we may turn our backs on that which we are uniquely prepared to fulfill, i.e., an awareness of the grace of God in enabling us and our parishioners to respond positively to life as a means toward but not a substitute for specific specialized processes.

The variations on the theme of being too quick to refer are quite numerous. There are times when we, as clergy, sell ourselves short, being unwilling or unable to affirm our own strength and resources. It is patently false modesty for us to defer when there is no valid basis for deferring. Through the years as I have had occasion to participate in certification processes both in the Association for Clinical Pastoral Education and the American Association of Pastoral Counselors, one of the issues that has been high on my priority is whether the person can honestly certify himself or herself. This is not designed to suggest or promote some sort of self-aggrandizement; it is to affirm that unless and until a person is able to "own"

---

[5]John 5:6, RSV.
[6]Vernon Johnson, *I'll Quit Tomorrow* (San Francisco, CA: Harper & Row, 1980).

professional strength and competence along with an awareness of limitations, that person is in some sense unfit for ministry.

From the polar opposite perspective, there are ministers who delay referral overlong. There is here the same sort of subtle unwillingness to face reality as observed in the situation of those who refer too quickly. For some there is the misguided notion that faith is—or should be—adequate for any and all human problems. Most of us have deplored this attitude on the part of some of our brothers and sisters in certain sects which resist any and all medical interventions and who discount the positive value in psychotherapy on the basis that certain therapists are not "religious people." One can admire the zeal of such persons but raise question about their judgement.

But having stated this extreme form of resistance to working with colleagues in the clinical spheres, there yet remains for all of us to be aware of subtle ways this point of view tends to beset us in one form or another. Who of us in the clergy has not at some time or other felt as though we were " second-class citizens" when it comes to dealing with human suffering? The competence of our colleagues in medicine, in psychiatry and psychology, in social work and vocational counseling has often tended to intimidate many of us and blind us to our own pastoral resources and skills. One of the subtle responses to this sense of being intimidated is our incorporating the vocabularies of these disciplines as our own. We have known (have been?) ministers who became adept in speaking of complexes and neuroses, of unconscious and subconscious, of behavioral patterns and personal resistances; we have known (have been?) those who were more familiar with the latest approach to therapy than with new developments in theology; we have known (have been?) those who felt somewhat uncomfortable with prayer or scripture in pastoral conversations and tended to avoid all "God talk" in working with persons. And woe betide us when we are more familiar with DSM III than with Scripture!

The variations on this theme are as subtle and as pervasive as the variations on the deference ploy. Through these and other stratagems we have sought to become (or appear) omnicompetent, and thus under no necessity to enlist the skill and experience of those who do "not follow with us."[7] In so doing, we found ourselves in danger of causing more harm than good, and sacrificing the well being of our parishioners on the altar of our own egos. The tragic outcome of the threats to our personal and professional competence is not only the perpetuation of human hurt but also the loss of our own integrity and identity.

When we move away from these two polar responses to referral, the question still remains regarding the indices which suggest referral. Most discussions I have read or heard put the focus on the situation of the person involved; and there is certainly a great deal to be said for the validity of this type of consideration. At the same time I am convinced that the primary indices are those to be explored in the person of the parishioner. As set forth in the 1960's discussion, these indices turn on significant limitations which may be found in the minister, limitations which may in some sense or other be functions of the situation but from whatever cause strongly indicate that referral is needed. Incidentally, following the elaboration of these factors, it is gratifying to see how many other writers in the field of pastoral care have incorporated them into their own consideration. The three limitations are (1) time, (2) skill, and (3) emotional reserve or stability. Since these are spelled out in some detail in my book on referral,[8] my purpose here is simply to elaborate on them briefly as a means for reminders in working with persons in trouble.

In regard to time, there are many instances when the minister is quite competent by reason of study and experience to deal with many of the difficult issues of life; nevertheless, it would be a poor stewardship of time for him or her to do so. The parish minister's primary task is focused on preaching, teaching, administration and pastoral care. Pastoral care, in this context, is the incorporating of the grace of God into the on-going issues of life, the common ventures such as birth, childhood, adolescence, young-adulthood, marriage, middle-age illness, aging and death. These personal situations are, to some extent, part and parcel of all of our lives although one or more of them may never confront all of us. As the minister makes available the means of grace through whatever appropriate fashion in the care of the people, little time is "left over" for "in-depth counseling." Many a minister has discovered, belatedly, that the calendar

---

[7]Luke 9:49, RSV.
[8]Oglesby, *Ibid.,* pp. 36ff.

becomes filled with week-to-week counseling appointments, leaving no opportunity for calling in the homes of parishioners, hospital visitation, and the maintenance of structures for day-to-day living in the lives of parishioners. Thus, although the minister may be quite prepared to do long-term counseling, referral is indicated to some community pastoral counseling service or similar group precisely because of the variety of things to be done in the parish. And, for all of us, the finding of ourselves gravitating toward time in the study, time in the counseling room, time in the administrative affairs of the congregation to the neglect of other matters gives serious cause for reassessing our priorities. In such circumstance, a careful look at the calendar over time can be quite revealing as to what (and why) we are avoiding and what steps are necessary to fulfill our whole ministry.

The variations of this theme are many but the basic point is clear. It is not helpful to vitiate one's schedule of caring for the whole people of God simply because one has the skill to do so in emergency. The laying hold on available resources for ministering to human suffering is one of the most significant dimensions of ministry. Admittedly, the geographical location of the parish presents issues and problems in terms of some types of resource. Nevertheless, the rapidity of modern transportation puts all or most of us in touch with specialized services; and we do our people no favor by neglecting this dimension of ministry.

In the second, referral is indicated when the minister has a limitation of skill or experience. Many clergy are able to work—at least for awhile—with persons whose distress is severe. The crucial question for us is, "Have I been down this road before and do I understand the meaning of the data which are being presented verbally or behaviorally?" If the answer is "yes," then it is possible for specialized ministry to be performed on a limited basis. Many ministers today have had extensive experience in hospitals and mental health facilities and are well qualified to deal with human misery. But the matter is governed by reference to the first limitation; *i.e.* time. One possible solution that I have observed among qualified colleagues is to designate a definite block of time for such purposes, perhaps four hours a week on Monday morning and limit their long-term counseling to those hours. This means, of course, that over time only a relatively few persons can be seen. But the regimen has been perceived as beneficial for the minister in keeping in touch with the pervasive dimensions of human suffering at a depth level and thus being potentially more sensitive to those human ills which are of less pervasive nature. No hard and fast rule can be identified. But the basic consideration is the balancing of the whole scope of ministry against this one particular area of competence.

Incidentally, the same principles apply whatever the special interest and competence may be. All of us know some ministers who spend an inordinate amount of time in the study working through intricate theological issues and preparing scholarly articles for journals along with the publication of books. Such activities preclude much time for pastoral care and referral seems to be the only answer. There is much to commend study and writing in ministry; but the issue here also turns on balance. Each of us has gifts and interests; the crux of the matter is the way we follow these creative dimensions of ourselves without neglecting the "whole counsel of God."

The third limitation which indicates the necessity for referral is quite personal rather than strictly professional. When I discussed this factor in 1966, I was unable to find a word or a term which would adequately describe it. The designation given above, "limitation of emotional reserve or security," still is about as close as I can come; but I am not happy with it. "Time" and "skill" are clear-cut and descriptive. "Emotional reserve or security" is not. In 1966, I asked whether anyone could improve on the matter. And, although—as noted— many writers have made use of these three categories, the designation of a term has apparently eluded us all. Of course, someone may have devised such a term and it has escaped me. In any event, I am still "looking" and welcome any suggestions .

Even without a concise term, the concept is easily recognized in our own ministries. There are times in the lives of all of us wherein certain issues or situations press in upon us with such force that we are unable to be objective. This has to do with matters that are still unresolved in our own lives to such an extent that we find ourselves dealing with our agenda rather than with the agenda of the parishioners. By a similar token, there are times and circumstances in our lives when we find ourselves personally enmeshed in the lives of the parishioners to the extent that we cannot maintain our appropriate perspective in terms of what is happening to them. This relates to the time-worn dictum that no physician "treats" family members, just as no surgeon ever operates on someone whose life is essential to his or her own. Any of us could come up with an exception to the matter; nevertheless, the basic thrust is clear. Our own lives are inevitably involved in the process—as is appropriate; but when the involvement is intense, then our competence is diminished.

There is another dimension to this index for referral and that is the situational circumstance that may be our own at the time. At particular points in the lives of all of us we are "drained" by reason of stress, anxiety, overt or convert pressure, the list runs on. In such times we do parishioners no service to act as if we can be available to them in their trouble. To start walking "through the valley of the shadow" with a parishioner only to reach the point where our own struggles incapacitate us to continue is a poorly devised attempt to be caring. There are, of course, those times when we do not assess ourselves accurately and find ourselves coming too close to the brink to be of help. Nevertheless, it is usual that we know from the outset that we are vulnerable; and it is a matter of caring not to proffer more that we can produce. We can provide pastoral care on another occasion—to the same person or persons in similar situation. But for now the burden is too great, and we do well to acknowledge it. My own experience is that although this type of event is disappointing to ourselves and to the parishioner, they tend to understand and welcome a suggestion that they allow someone else to bear the burden with them just now.

How to Refer

All that we have said until now assumes that our primary concern is that the parishioner receive the most responsible and constructive help available and not that we will, necessarily, be the primary source of that help. In a word, our hope is that the person be helped rather than seeing ourselves as the only best channel for that help. Once this has been resolved in our own thinking, the process of referral is set in proper perspective.

It is essential that care be taken lest it seem that we are dismissing the persons at a crucial phase of their lives. Such a perception is easily interpreted as rejection; and people in pain are particularly sensitive at that point. The best way of avoiding any notion of rejection is to assure that the process of referral becomes a "partnership" or "corporate" event. The minister's primary commitment, as noted above, is that the person find resources; and if the minister is not the prime provider of these services he or she, nonetheless, is eager to enable the parishioner to lay hold on them. Thus the paradigm phrase is not "you go to such and such a person or facility," but "let us discover together the person or facility that will be of most value to you." This avoids the pitfall that the minister may seem to "take over" the person's life on the one hand or dismiss the person out of hand on the other. Rather, they—together—move toward the healing that the parishioner so sorely needs.

One asset that the minister has is a knowledge of what is available and some assurance that this or that person or service is effective. Since the parishioner often does not have access to this information, the minister becomes a resource for "where to look." There are times when the minister finds it necessary to make a preliminary call, although my own experience is that far more can be accomplished when the parishioner is able to do that. If the minister is to make the call, it seems essential, except under the most extraordinary of circumstances, that the call be made in the presence of the parishioner. Nothing more than the bare details of setting up the appointment need be included. The colleague is then in a position—together with the parishioner—to delve into the disturbing matters toward moving toward release. A simple word such as, "John Wilson is experiencing some personal distresses in which he and I believe that you and he can best determine the situation and what is needed if that seems well to you." To be sure, on many occasions the area of the distress may be mentioned, such as "having trouble sleeping," or "experiencing worry about a teenage child, " or the like; in any instance it seems more productive if details are left to the conversation between the parishioner and the person to whom the parishioner is referred.

Where to Refer

In the first edition of the 1960's book, I listed a general category of places and resources useful to the minister in referral. These included groups such as psychiatrists, physicians, family counselors, and the list ran on. I also noted community organizations, private groups, and particular services that were available. Wherever possible I listed addresses and phone numbers where information could be obtained.

As would be expected, the list was "out of date" before the ink was dry! Thus, in a second edition some ten years later, I included an update of referral resources. Expectedly, that met the same fate. The scene changes regularly as new groups replace outmoded ones, and as new interests become the focus of specialized help. The comments here are of a generic nature rather than specific.

In the first part of this article I noted the obvious kinds of collegial resources that would certainly be known by most clergy. These included professional persons, volunteers, private organizations, and members of the People of God. In regard to specifics, in most urban areas such groups as United Way or Community Mental Health Organizations have available lists or data about resources useful to ministers. Moreover, pastoral organizations such as CC of APHA, AAPC, ACPE, NACC, and the like,[9] publish membership data which may be helpful to clergy in finding resources in areas removed from their own. In like fashion, many ministers rely on personal acquaintances nearby and remote for suggestions and evaluations of this or that resource. Having been in the Richmond, Virginia, area for more than three decades and having colleagues in the surrounding areas I have often been asked for names of persons or groups by clergy in nearby states as well as across the country. Each of us can profit by the first-hand knowledge of groups or persons that is available to colleagues with closer contacts than we possess. In my own instance, when asked for a referral resource in a distant area, I probably will not know a specific person or group there but I can put the individual in touch with someone who does.

Ongoing Ministry Following Referral

There are some general guidelines that are helpful to us when we refer a person or a family to some specialized group or person. Perhaps the primary "rule of thumb" is that we make no attempt to maintain a specific "professional" relationship with the parishioner. This means that we will in no sense engage in some sort of

---

[9]CC of APHA stands for The College of Chaplains of the American Protestant Health Association, 1701 East Woodfield Road, Suite 311, Schaumburg, Illinois 60195; AAPC stands for The American Association of Pastoral Counselors, 9508a Lee Highway, Fairfax, Virginia 22031; ACPE stands for The Association for Clinical Pastoral Education, 1549 Clairmont Road, Suite 103, Decatur, Georgia 30033; and NACC stands for the National Association of Catholic Chaplains, 3257 South Lake Drive, Milwaukee, Wisconsin 53207-0905. Other such listings may be found on the back cover of *The Journal of Pastoral Care*.

"treatment plan" during the time the parishioner is being helped by the referral resource. Of course this does not mean that we break off our pastoral relationships with the parishioners. It does mean that we refrain from delving into the details of the treatment process.

When referral is made, it is customary to note that there is no assurance that all will be well; and if difficulties arise the parishioner may wish to consult regarding seeking help elsewhere. But the issue is complex. It is not helpful for the minister to encourage parishioners to retreat at the first point of struggle or to seek "rescue" from personal responsibility. The ordinary constructive procedure is to encourage the person to continue so that the process may receive a "fair trial." Even so, all of us know that there is no absolute assurance that any professional relationship will always prove beneficial; and our concern for our parishioners is that they find the appropriate resource, not simply that our referral guarantees success.

Throughout, our pastoral care and concern for the parishioners remains. It is not helpful to pry into what is happening now to make repeated suggestions for process. But the "pastor - people" relationships in worship, in study, in service, in recreation are important. Indeed, these types of relationships are the ones which endure following the times with the referral resource even as they were crucial prior to the referral. The imagery is one of ongoing nurture before and after particularized emergency nurture. It is in this sense that genuine pastoral care is provided.

Confidentiality

One final word in regard to confidentiality and privileged communication. All of us have been sensitive to these matters through the years, and rightly so. In recent times as our society has become more litigious we naturally tend to pay particular attention to that which is legal alongside that which is ethical or moral. One factor that is essential for our understanding is that the communication "privilege" is always that of the parishioner. Neither clergy nor other groups have privilege in disclosing or refusing to disclose data. It is certain that various customs, whether codified or not, have often assigned to priests, ministers and rabbis certain immunities from having to reveal confidential material. But what is involved in such matters is the privilege of the parishioner to limit disclosure. Where this becomes a matter of law, the clergyperson may elect to undergo penalty or imprisonment; but to do so is to act in behalf of the parishioner's rights and wishes and not because of one's own.

The fundamental issue always is the welfare of the parishioner and of other persons. How can the greatest good be served is the matter that confronts us at such points; and to this sort of question there often seems no absolute answer. "We ought to obey God rather than men"[10] is clear-cut on its face. But the troublesome questions remain as to who decides what "obeying God" means in this or that circumstance. Few of us would plead an individualistic interpretation in this matter; rather, holding that there is corporate wisdom that can transcend individual decision, most of us find constructive help in consultation with colleagues even though—in the end—we are responsible for our own decisions and actions.

Conclusion

Referral is a meaningful aspect of ministry as we seek to discover and effect along with parishioners the most creative resources for dealing with the struggles of life. We rejoice that we are not alone, that professional skills and competences are available to meet the traumas of life and personal relationships. At the same time, we rejoice that we, as clergy, have access to resources of grace which, although available to and often affirmed by nonclerical persons, comprise our primary responsibility in dealing with human need and suffering. This means that when we see these spiritual gifts being manifested by and in those not of the "cloth" we rejoice and have no need to introject ourselves into the relationship. But it also means that we, alone, are responsible for being certain that these resources are available and are in no position to find fault with colleagues when they do not emphasize them. It is in this holistic sense of resources for human need that we, along with colleagues, enable persons to lay hold on the means of grace—and live.

---

[10]Acts 5:29, KJV.

Pastoral Care of the Mentally Ill:
A Congregational Perspective*

CLARK S. AIST, Ph.D.,
Director, Protestant Chaplain Activities,
Saint Elizabeths Hospital, Washington, DC 20032

R endering pastoral care to persons suffering from severe mental disorders is an increasingly prominent dimension of ministry in the congregational setting today. The movement to "deinstitutionalize" the nation's mentally ill and to provide for their treatment in the least restrictive environment possible is making the community the permanent home for all but the most seriously impaired. More and more the recovering mental patient is the person in front of us at the grocery check-out, or behind us at the movie theater, or across from us at McDonald's, or beside us at worship.

The importance of the diverse resources of church and temple in providing enlightened care and humane treatment for significantly troubled persons has been cited frequently and cannot be overestimated. In the United States, for example, clergy outnumber psychiatrists by nearly ten to one and are much more equitably distributed geographically than any other mental health professional. A consistent finding over the past two decades indicates that approximately 40 percent of persons seeking outside help with emotional distress turn first to the clergy, a figure considerably higher than for the next largest group, physicians.[1]

There is also evidence that a growing number of persons who seek assistance from priests, ministers and rabbis manifest symptoms

---

*The views expressed in this article are those of the author and do not reflect the views or policies of Saint Elizabeths Hospital or the U.S. Department of Health and Human Services.

[1]Gerald Gurin, *et al., Americans View Their Mental Health* (New York, NY: Basic Books, 1960), pp. 305-307; R.A. Kulka, Joseph Veroff, and E. Douvan, "Social Class and the Use of Professional Help for Personal Problems," *Journal of Health and Social Behavior,* 1979, Vol. 20, pp. 2-17.

of major psychiatric illness.[2] For some, this is connected with a first (and perhaps only) occurrence of a severe mental disorder. For others, the symptoms represent a resurfacing of an underlying disturbance that is periodically exacerbated by increased environmental stress or failure to continue medication. For still others, the bizarre manifestations indicate a more or less constant state of profound maladjustment which remains relatively untouched by available treatment measures. As we shall see, each of these groups has distinctive needs and must be approached differently. In attending to these persons pastorally, congregation-based clergy occupy a strategic position as front-line caregivers for those who are among the community's most needy and disabled citizens. Sketching the historical context of this aspect of ministry and a framework of principles and methods that may be useful in carrying it out is the objective of this article.

An Ancient Role Reclaimed

Affirming an expanded function for congregational clergy in caring pastorally for the profoundly troubled is not to suggest the assumption of a new role but the reclamation of an ancient role, honed to fit contemporary needs. It is important to remember that during vast expanses of human history treaters of mental illness and priests of religion were one and the same. The intervention of God (or gods) in human affairs to punish and heal, and alternately the intrusion of diabolical spirits to tempt and torment, were prevailing constructs for understanding and alleviating mental disorders.

Without doubt, Christian beliefs and practices did much to elevate public attitudes toward the "lunatic" and injected a kindlier tone in their treatment. During the late Middle Ages and Renaissance, however, a resurgence of crude notions of demon possession and magical superstition occurred. An ominous linkage was forged between witchcraft and mental illness; within two centuries, several hundred thousand demented persons were executed in France and Germany alone under religious auspices.[3]

---

[2]While I know of no scientific study that confirms this observation, clinical experience, case evidence, and anecdotal reports all strongly support its veracity.

[3]Gregory Zilboorg, *The Medical Man and The Witch During The Renaissance* (Baltimore, MD.: The Johns Hopkins Press, 1935).

It was not until the eighteenth century Enlightenment that medicine as a whole and the treatment of insanity in particular was purged of supernaturalism and infused with a spirit of scientific inquiry. Inspired by attitudes of humane concern and optimism regarding therapeutic outcome, new hospitals for the insane were built at public expense all over Europe and America. These hospitals undoubtedly conferred significant curative benefits upon those who inhabited them, especially when compared with earlier custodial practices; but there were drawbacks as well. One was the uprooting of the "mental patient" from his or her family, neighborhood, and local religious congregation in order to "take cure" in a far-off asylum. *As a consequence, pastoral care for the profoundly troubled became increasingly disjoined from the day to day functions of community ministers, priests, and rabbis.*

"Refer psychotics" has long been the predominant advice given to local clergy.[4] With the widespread return of the mentally ill to the community over the past fifteen years, however, this position is no longer tenable. The stage now seems to be set for neighborhood clergy once again to exercise their ancient pastoral authority in relation to the seriously mentally impaired, not surely as appeasers of gods or expellers of demons, but as contemporary "soul-healers" wedding insights and methods from both theology and the behavioral sciences.

The Present Context

If pastoral care for the mentally ill in local congregations reclaims a traditional role rather than establishes a new one, the *context* in which this role is being implemented today is characterized by a considerable amount of change and novelty. The keystone in this veritable "arch of change" can undoubtedly be traced to the introduction of the phenothiazines and anti-depressant drugs in the treatment of psychotic disorders during the mid-1950s. The elements of innovation connected directly or indirectly with this phenomenon are kaleidoscopic. The new medications not only made it possible successfully to treat many otherwise "hopeless" patients, but enabled large numbers to leave inpatient facilities tor a spectrum of residen-

---

[4]Paul C. Hollinger, *Pastoral Care of Severe Emotional Disorders* (New York, NY: Irvington publishers, Inc., 1985), p. 3.

tial arrangements in the community where supervision was cali-
brated to meet rehabilitative needs.

A related development has been a diversification in the overall
system for delivering psychiatric services into what now includes
community mental health centers (approximately 800 nationwide);
psychiatric units in general hospitals; nursing homes for the psychi-
atrically impaired elderly; and a growing number of corporation-
owned, private psychiatric hospitals. Public mental hospitals, the
once powerful flagships of the nation's mental health program, now
treat only those who cannot afford private care or whose illnesses are
sufficiently disabling or protracted to warrant long-term hospitalization.

As the effects of these changes accumulate, the result will be an
even larger population of persons recovering from mental disorders
who reside in the community.[5] Although laudable in theory, the
practical effects of deinstitutionalization have often been mixed.
Some communities, themselves already underserved, have simply not
been prepared to receive returning mental patients. Many persons
have had no alternative but to join thorazine ghettos or to swell the
ranks of the homeless.

A quite different line of change which is at least partially traceable to the introduction of psychotropic medications is the historic
shift in American psychiatry away from psychodynamic perspectives
toward more biologically oriented views, sometimes referred to as
the "remedicalization" of psychiatry.[6] The integration of Freudian
psychoanalysis into the mainstream theory and practice of psychiatry
during the first half of this century had powerful ramifications for
the fledgling pastoral care and counseling movement. Both fields
were able to address each other appreciatively using the "dialect of
psychodynamics" in what Edgar Draper has called a "romance" that

---

[5]The much cited decline in the population of U.S. mental hospitals beginning
in 1956 was in all probability the first reversal of an upward trend that spanned no
less than two centuries. Ever since physicians assumed primary responsibility for
the care of the mentally ill from ministers of religion several hundred years ago,
the general trend in hospital-based treatment had been upward. It is ironic that a
reversal of this trend should be accompanied by (1) increased pessimism (or real-
ism) with regard to treatment outcomes for many mental disorders, and (2) increased opportunities for community-based religious personnel and agencies to
resume participation in the care of those with serious disabilities.

[6]Melvin Sabshin, "On Remedicalization and Holism," *Psychiatry in Psychosomatics,*
1977, Vol. 18, No. 4, pp. 7-8.

was "intense, exciting, and productive for many years." [7] The decline in analytic orientation and the ascendency of neurobiological and behaviorist views has caused what amounts to a hermeneutic crisis in the relationship between mainline psychiatry and the clinical pastoral disciplines.

Psychiatry has responded to the new pluralism in its ranks by adopting an atheoretical, descriptive approach to diagnosis (best illustrated by DSM III and DSM III R) and a highly eclectic approach to treatment. Data are constantly being collected to determine empirically what methods are most beneficial and cost effective. Thus a clinician might well use analytic methods to treat Hysterical Neurosis, behavioral methods to treat Phobic Disorders, and a combination of chemotherapy and brief hospitalization followed by supportive psychotherapy to treat Schizophrenic Disorders.

One of the most far-reaching changes instigated by the discovery and use of symptom-suppressing drugs is the rapidly accumulating body of knowledge about the neurological, genetic and biochemical factors that influence mental health and illness. Researchers now have evidence to hypothesize that an excess of certain brain chemicals (like dopamine) are associated with schizophranic-type symptoms; deficiencies in others (serotonin and norepinephrine) appear to be connected with depression. In addition, studies using computerized tomography (CT) positron emission tomography (PET)[8] have discovered a variety of structural abnormalities in the brains of persons with schizophrenia, while twin studies have demonstrated a definite but imprecise genetic influence in the development of this disorder. Although the ultimate causes of all but a few mental illnesses are not definitively known, these and other findings have convinced many investigators that most of the affective and schizophrenic disorders are, in fact, genetically influenced diseases of the brain.

Deinstitutionalization, diversification, remedicalization, biologization, psychopharmacologization. These are the complex phe-

---

[7]Edgar Draper and Bevan Steadman, "Assessment in Pastoral Care," in Robert J. Wicks, Richard D. Parsons and Donald E. Capps (Eds.), *Clinical Handbook of Pastoral Counseling* (New York, NY: Paulist Press 1985), p. 119.

[8]These are techniques which enable researchers to visualize the function of various structures in living human brains by tracking radioactive elements as they pass through the brain's arteries.

nomena which characterize today's mental health environment in which congregational clergy are increasingly assuming new responsibilities for those with severe mental disorders.

Preparatory Steps

Implementing an effective ministry of pastoral care with significantly distressed persons requires careful preparation by the congregation and its spiritual leader. Preparation is not so much a prior activity that ceases when the main task begins, but, as used here, represents a cluster of necessary preconditions which must be continually sustained.

Of foremost importance is the clergyperson's own *personal and professional preparation* in acquiring (and maintaining) the necessary knowledge, skills, and personal resources to carry out this aspect of ministry. A reasonable level of competence can be achieved by combinations of academic or workshop courses, on-going case consultation, short-term or extended CPE units, and regular peer support activities. Persons preparing for specialty positions such as full-time program director in a multi-staff congregation should have not less than a year of CPE in a mental health setting. Essential areas of knowledge include the nature and symptoms of psychotic illnesses, methods for assessing the needs of the chronically troubled, goals and principles of supportive counseling, the clinical use of religious and spiritual resources, and the types and effects of common psychotropic medicines and other treatment methods.

Of critical significance is a sustained opportunity to visit with psychotic persons *under supervision* so that clergypersons can apply their cognitive understandings in concrete pastoral encounters, can grapple with their own personal strengths and limitations, can understand the effects of their attitudinal responses (both positive and negative). Without the discipline of practice under supervision, emotional legacies stemming from misinformation, unexamined personal experience, and centuries of communal prejudice and stigma can often transform initial sympathy and good will into fear, mistrust, and unintentional efforts to get the disturbed person "out of the way."

A second area of preparation is the formation and maintenance of *a support network* to assist the clergyperson in implementing this special type of ministry. Regardless of how extensive one's initial training or the quality of one's natural gifts, no one should engage in pastoral ministry with profoundly troubled persons as a loner. The risk of becoming over-extended, overwhelmed with needs, and burned out is simply too great. A primary and indispensable element in the clergyperson's support network is a qualified and experienced psychiatric consultant whose role is not so much to "treat" people, but to assist the clergyperson in best utilizing the resources available to the benefit of the troubled individual. In this relationship the consultant will need to steer a middle course between the scylla of unduly minimizing the clergyperson's contributions and the charybdis of making the clergyperson over into his or her own image (*e.g.* a "junior" psychiatrist). There is considerable evidence that many psychiatrists are open and eager to enter into just such a positive collaborative arrangement.

Another essential resource for the clergyperson's support network is the chaplaincy staffs of the locality's mental health facilities. From their position inside the mental health system they can provide extensive information on such matters as commitment and discharge procedures, the location of specialized resources, where help can be found in an immediate crisis, and assistance in the sometimes nettlesome problem of finding an effective psychiatric consultant.

Mental health chaplains are also a chief source of education for continuing competency through such offerings as formal CPE programs, workshops, weekly support and discussion groups, and on-going pastoral case conferences.

Additional significant network elements may also include other clergy peers who are engaged in similar pastoral care activities, consortia of local congregations which combine their resources in providing food or shelter or clothing, and lay persons within the congregation who have been specially trained to assist in particular facets of the pastoral case program. The important point is that a larger support network for the clergyperson is needed so that all the ingredients of the community's religious and mental health resources can be effectively mobilized as needed in the effort to assist the non-hospitalized mentally ill.

A third area of preparation is *creating a climate of acceptance* in the life of the congregation. Any effort to aid persons suffering from psychotic disorders in a community setting will be hassled by un-founded fears, multi-generational distortions, myths, and prejudices. Religious congregations are not an exception. One of the most common manifestations of this problem is the tendency to fit all mentally troubled persons into a stereotypic mold ("They'll be all right. Just treat them like little children.")

Creating a climate of acceptance must be done intentionally, but in large measure can be successfully accomplished only sponta-neously. By this is meant seizing opportunities whenever they ap-pear—in sermons, in business sessions, during pastoral visits, in de-ciding the content of programs, in casual conversation, and through many other circumstances—to demonstrate how similar are our re-spective problems and how much more alike we all are than differ-ent. The emphasis is on spontaneity because this understanding of our common humanity must pervade everything from the content of one's prayers to one's commentary on public events involving men-tally disturbed persons. Intentional efforts have their place too, how-ever, and can include such activities as forums led by mental health leaders and conducting special educational units on relevant topics. Especially effective is the effort by some congregations to define their mission in the community in especially inclusive terms ("showing hospitality to the stranger," " serving the 'least of these' as Christ incognito," *etc.*). Above all, the clergyperson must convey a sensitive and informed respect for the dignity of all persons, a com-passion for their problems, a mature tolerance of his or her own short-comings, and an unshakable commitment to regard all confi-dences as sacred.

A final area of preparation would be the *articulation of an overall goal* (or goals). Though each clergyperson and congregation will ex-press it differently, the core intention will be to enable the troubled individual to experience the "abundant life" to the extent possible by making optimum use of the resources available in the religious con-gregation and in the community. Regardless of the words used, the statement of goals should (1) represent a collaboratively arrived at understanding between the clergyperson and the congregation, (2) highlight the uniquely pastoral dimensions of helping endeavor,[9]

---

[9]While perhaps not an absolute safeguard in the present litigious environment, it is important that the primary aim of offering "pastoral" care to the emotionally distressed person is clearly enunciated even if it is recognized that such care may

(3) stress the linkage function in facilitating the use of a broad range of resource options, and (4) make provision for regular review and up-dating.

The Helping Process

The first major step in the helping process should consist of a careful assessment of the distressed individual. Pastoral assessment has been discussed from a variety of perspectives,[10] and it is essential in order to avoid the trap of behaving as though pastoral care, like patent medicines of old, provides the same remedy for every problem.

The purpose of the pastoral assessment (like diagnosis in medicine) is not to fix a label, but to help the clergyperson answer the question: "What among the available resources can best meet this person's needs?"

Ascertaining whether the individual's symptoms of distress are of psychotic proportions[11] is one of the first determinations to be made. Psychotic symptoms are thoughts, feelings or behaviors which give evidence of a gross impairment in the individual's ability accurately to perceive and evaluate inner or external realities. Hearing voices, certainty of being poisoned, insistence upon having caused a natural catastrophe, each without confirming external evidence, are examples of psychotic symptoms.

Generally speaking, congregational clergy will likely encounter three forms of psychosis with some degree of frequency. These are the Schizophrenic Disorders, certain of the Affective Disorders and certain of the Organic Brain Disorders, to use the language of DSM-III.[12] The clergyperson will want to acquire a reasonably clear grasp

---

have a saluatory medical benefit. The pastoral nature and aim of the care should be described in such a way that clearly distinguishes it from outpatient psychiatric care and other physician supervised interventions.

[10]Edgar Draper, *Psychiatry and Pastoral Care* (Englewood Cliffs, NJ: Prentice-Hall, Inc., 1965); Paul W. Pruyser, *The Minister as Diagnostician* (Philadelphia, PA: Westminster Press, 1976); Wayne Oates, *The Religious Care of the Psychiatric Patient* (Philadelphia, PA: Westminster Press, 1978); and Hollinger, *op, cit.*

[11]It is helpful here to keep in mind the distinction between the term *psychotic* that refers to symptoms (*e.g.* thoughts, feelings or behavior) which are characterized by a gross impairment in one's ability to assess reality accurately, and the term *psychosis* that refers to any of several illnesses sometime during the course of which an individual will manifest "psychotic" symptoms.

of these syndromes and the symptom patterns associated with them (as well as other categories of psychosis).[13] This will not be, however, for the purpose of rendering precision diagnoses which is clearly a psychiatric function. The clergyperson is far more interested in assessing whether the psychotic symptoms (whatever the underlying disorder) have recently appeared for the first time, or whether they reflect a recurrence of a previously known and treated disorder, or whether they represent a rather stabilized pattern of profound maladjustment that treatment has not yet resolved.

The Pastoral Assessment Interview. The clergyperson obtains the information needed to make a relevant assessment by conducting a pastoral assessment interview with the distressed person. Essentially, this is a conversational process in which the interviewee-congregant is assisted in telling the story of his or her present troubles. The process begins as the individual is asked to describe, as much as possible, the problem or problems that bring him or her to see the minister, priest or rabbi. Paul Hollinger, a psychiatrist who is also theologically trained, aptly summarizes the core information needed as follows:

> Particularly important are any precipitating factors in the current episode, previous similar episodes, previous psychiatric hospitalizations (for what reasons, what diagnosis, how long) and recent medical procedures (organic syndromes are often associated with psychotic symptoms). Also essential is knowing what, if any, medications the person is taking and for how long, for many psychotropic and general medical drugs can cause psychotic symptoms. In addition an acquaintance with psychotropic medications can alert the pastor to the general diagnostic impressions of the previous physicians.[14]

If in the natural unfolding of the story the person does not cover (or cover sufficiently) some of the information needed, the clergyperson should not hesitate to ask specific questions. Among the important questions which must be answered during the interview if at all possible are "Why is help being sought?" and "Why is it

---

[12]American Psychiatric Association, *Diagnostic and Statistical Manual of Mental Disorders* (Third Edition), Washington, D.C., 1980. This is the most widely used and authoritative resource in the United States for the classification of mental disorders.

[13]There are several other more rarely seen categories of psychoses such as Paranoid Disorders, atypical psychoses, and the autistic disorders of infancy and childhood. More detailed descriptions and symptoms manifestations may be found in DSM-III and in the DSM III R.

[14]Hollinger, *op. cit.*, p. 53.

being sought *now?"* Included also are questions about suicidal or homicidal thoughts, plans or intentions especially when depression seems a prominent feature. In cases where events are especially painful and memory seems to be vague, it is sometimes helpful to ask the person to recount what they have been occupied with over the last two or three days. Often the repetitive "And then what happened?" turns up key information that sheds important new light on the situation. (Such a procedure, however, should not be forced on a person, especially if the matter appears to be too difficult for them to talk about. "If it's not too painful for you. . ." should generally precede a request of this kind.)

Other data will be useful once the circumstances surrounding the current episode have been explored, such as the individual's age, where he or she grew up, family background including siblings and relations to parents, how things went in school (and the extent of education), marital status and children, and vocation and work history. Of particular significance is the person's religious affiliation and faith history. Here the clergyperson secures information on the extent of involvement and participation in ecclesial activities as well as the individual's private beliefs and views on religious subjects *(e.g.* prayer, good and evil, knowing the will of God, *etc.)* .

Information on religious involvement and faith history will have several important values in the assessment process. First, it will indicate the extent to which religious ideas (1) represent an idiosyncratic expression of the individual's mental disorder (God has selected them for a special mission), (2) represent valid communal beliefs which are being responded to in an inappropriate or exaggerated manner due to the illness (morbid guilt for having violated dietary laws), (3) represent beliefs within a communally shared range but which reveal a theme that is skewed in terms of life need or experience (persistent images of God, church, Bible, *etc.,* as conveying judgmental legalism), (4) represent impoverishment of belief because of lack of instruction, or (5) represent a communally shared pattern with no discernible skewing in relation to the illness. Second, information about the interviewee's religious involvement and beliefs should give some clues as to whether discussion of or focus on religious matters will promote resistance, antagonism, tangentialness or openness, genuineness, self-disclosure, *etc.* Third, a meaningful religious assessment should indicate how the individual may be prepared to appropriate various components of the congregation's religious life and activity (*e.g.* whether they are ready "to sit one on the right hand and one on the left," or whether they will need to "follow afar off," at least for a time).

Pulling the Data Together. The next major step in the helping process is pulling the assessment data together into an overall evaluative picture. Is there evidence of psychotic illness? Are ideas sufficiently bizarre and incoherent as to represent delusions? Are they believed to be *really* true? Is there an exaggerated mood state, either high or low? Are the person's thoughts coherent and connected and do they seem to match his or her mood? Does the person show any sign of being disoriented—confusion as to who they are, where they are, or the time-frame they are living in? Is there evidence of memory loss—in a global sense or for recent events or for particular time periods, *etc.* ? Are there signs of alcohol or drug use of any type? Has anything like this happened before—when, where and what was done? Did a physical illness, surgery or hospitalization precede the emotional upset? Who composes the individual's family network and how are they involved? Is there an immediate danger of harm through suicide or homicide? Are voices urging infliction or injury to self or others? Does the individual's religious practices and beliefs represent an asset or a barrier?

As the clergyperson attempts to answer these questions from the assessment information, a picture will generally emerge that points to (1) the probability of a particular clinical syndrome, (2) a stage of illness somewhere along the continuum between initial onset and chronic symptom manifestation, (3) a reasonable estimation of danger to self or others, and (4) a tentative strategy for helping that can be proposed to the distressed person.

Matching Need With Helping Resources. Once the clergyperson has concluded that an individual does manifest psychotic symptoms, the next step is to decide which of three basic categories of pastoral approach may be best suited to their needs. These are heuristic groupings which transcend the DSM III diagnostic syndromes, and are based on the levels of help that the individual needs which the clergyperson and/or congregation can provide. The first category includes persons whose symptoms represent a first-time occurrence of a psychotic disorder or those whose disorders have not been previously treated. Typically these persons generate considerable alarm among family members and associates who recognize that a very dramatic (and often sudden) change has occurred. There is no history of prior hospitalization for a mental problem, nor any recollection of taking anti-psychotic medication. Even when there is evidence of prior mental disorder, however, the connection with the present episode may be tenuous *(e.g.* an individual, apparently recovered from a transient reactive psychosis during adolescence, now manifests psychotic symptoms after taking PCP.) There may or may not be evidence of a precipitating cause such as illicit drug use or severe malnutrition .

The functions of the clergyperson with individuals in this category of need are several. The first is to guide the person to a competent source of medical-psychiatric evaluation and treatment. Here the clergyperson will draw on his or her knowledge of the local mental health network, both public and private, to help locate the needed services. If the individual is unwilling to accept help, it may be necessary to assist the family or law enforcement personnel in securing an emergency evaluation, especially if the individual is hallucinating or gives evidence of suicidal or homicidal proclivities. An alliance arranged in advance with a trusted psychiatric colleague who could help in dealing with such emergencies would be invaluable. A second function of the clergyperson is to maintain a supportive pastoral relationship with the person while treatment is in process. Visits to an inpatient unit should be brief, affirming, hopeful but realistic, and supportive. A significant ministry to family members may be needed at this time to deal with feelings of guilt and shame, and to discuss ways that they can be most helpful.[15] A third function with persons in this category is to be pastorally available during the post-treatment period for a ministry which may range from friendly situational pastoral conversations (on the street, after worship, *etc.)* to regularly scheduled pastoral counseling in collaboration with those responsible for the aftercare.

The second basic category of need in terms of pastoral care for persons with psychotic manifestations includes those whose present symptoms represent a recurrence of a previously known and treated

---

[15]The stress and pain experienced by families of the mentally ill are difficult to overestimate. The financial strain can be ruinous and the emotional strain highly disruptive to the family's stability. The clergyperson can offer the family objective caring, information regarding treatment options, a realistic view of their troubled family members, and a non-condemning acceptance of the anger, shame and love.

disorder. This group includes many relatively long-term, former mental patients now living in the community, often with a high degree of success and satisfaction—sometimes not. Generally, these are individuals whose symptoms are suppressed through psychotropic drugs. The reappearance of symptoms may accompany a failure to continue the prescribed medications (these often do have problematic side effects.) Or the symptoms may be due to a sudden increase in environmental stress (loss of a job, death of a loved one). Another possibility is that the person is experiencing a relapse or an intensification of the illness for any of a variety of reasons.

The clergyperson's functions with individuals in this category include relinking the person with his or her previous source of treatment, if at all possible. Usually the former patient, even when symptoms are active, is able to disclose previous hospitalizations, those responsible for their treatment, and their drug regimen. Much time and effort can be saved if the individual is able to return to the previous treatment source. Very often stabilization can be accomplished in outpatient status or with very brief hospitalization. Again some individuals will refuse help, and emergency examination measures may need to be followed. Following treatment and return to the community, many persons in this category can derive considerable benefit from group support, socialization and recreation activities. Often organized as a club in a church or synagogue and led by volunteers, these programs emphasize good health and hygiene, connectedness with a caring community (celebrating birthdays and holiday seasons and sharing griefs and troubles), meaningful activities (trips, crafts), and above all taking "meds." In some programs, medical follow-up is given concurrently during club meetings. Ongoing pastoral counseling is often indicated to maintain stable adjustment, but not with an emphasis on "uncovering" (encouraging self-disclosure, open expression of anger, transference, *etc.*) which may indeed be harmful to the psychotic patient. Much more useful is a supportive type of relationship "oriented toward improved reality testing, linkage with community resources, and symptom control through medication compliance."[16] When linked with the stability of regular religious rituals, this type of counseling can be very helpful.

---

[16]Robert E. Drake and David I. Sederer, "Inpatient Psychosocial Treatment of Chronic Schizophrenia Negative Effects and Current Guidelines," *Hospital and Community Psychiatry*, Vol. 37, No. 9, p. 898.

The third basic category of need involving pastoral care of persons with psychotic disorder includes individuals whose symptoms are associated with profound maladjustments that treatment has not resolved. These persons tend to be quite mobile and are heavily represented among the street population. Their symptoms are sometimes very florid in conversation, but because they tend not to talk to anybody and nobody talks to them, they are generally tolerated as not posing a danger to self or others. They usually do not have accessible families or to be open to treatment, perhaps because so much of what they have experienced has failed. Many gravitate to religious agencies for help, and a number of congregations have responded by developing a range of services.

The clergyperson's helping function with these persons is more apt to be group rather than individually oriented, and more related to survival elements than to social needs. Congregations have developed programs providing shelter, food, medical assistance, clothing and other essentials in response to their often desperate condition. These persons are often "obnoxiously ill" and churches with outreach ministries have found it necessary to establish firm rules about the use of church facilities, times to leave and return to the shelter area, *etc.* Some can be reached through counseling and persuaded to accept psychiatric treatment, but this is the exception, not the rule. Employment is generally precluded, but some have made adjustments in sheltered work experiences. A pastoral care that seeks to assure basic needs but remains ready to assist in other areas when possible, is perhaps the most feasible approach at present.

In reading these guidelines, some clergy will no doubt despair at the time and effort such a ministry could consume in an already crowded role agenda. While this is undoubtedly true, this author has been impressed again and again by what can be done over time through a small amount of intentional effort. An example is a clinically informed Lutheran pastor in Indiana who, in response to a challenge to give a "tithe" of his professional time for the mentally ill, succeeded within five years (1) to compile a detailed analysis of the mental health needs of the state and the potential contributions of the religious community, (2) to present his findings to the State Commissioner on Mental Health, (3) to become a member of the board of his local CMHC, (4) to volunteer his expertise in group pastoral counseling to demonstrate the feasibility of a chaplain position in the CMHC (which was later funded and filled), and (5) to organize in the newly constructed parish building where he serves a church-based aftercare program for mentally ill clients covering a three-county area![17] It is undoubtedly true that no one has the time to do all that needs to be done in this area. But with imagination and persistence, more can be accomplished than anyone would dream possible.

Conclusion

This article (1) has reviewed the historical role of religious institutions in the care of the mentally ill, (2) has summarized the present context in which community clergy are assuming an increasingly prominent position as pastoral caregivers for the deeply troubled, and (3) has offered guidelines for preparing and implementing a congregationally-based ministry of pastoral care for persons with severe mental disorders, including descriptions of the assessment and helping processes. Sending modern-day Legions to out-of-the-way wildernesses for protracted periods of time (like public mental hospitals) is a rapidly vanishing option in contemporary society. The growing presence of the mentally ill in our communities represents an unprecedented challenge and opportunity for the nation's churches and temples.

---

[17]Joseph M. Freeman, "Interface Between Congregation, Pastor, and CMHC Systems: A Local Understanding," *AMHC FORUM,* Vol. 35, No. 1, pp. 20-23.

Ritual in Pastoral Care

KENNETH R. MITCHELL, Ph. D.,
Pastoral Counseling Services,
564 N. E. Ravenna Blvd.,
Seattle, WA 98115

M any serious students of pastoral care, or of ritual, find any positive relationship between the two dubious at best. To begin a consideration of ritual in pastoral care, therefore, we need to remember how recent the mutual suspicion is.

Until about fifty years ago, rituals of church life were closely intertwined with pastoral care. The history of pastoral care paralleled the history of ritual (it could even be said that at times it *was* the history of ritual), for pastoral care was expressed, more often than not, in ritualized forms. After the apostolic era, pastoral responses to critical life situations took on, in many cases, a ritualized and formal character; pastoral responses to human situations were often judged appropriate or inappropriate by how faithfully they clove to established forms. That pattern held sway for much of Christian history.[1]

The last half-century has seen a major change, traceable to at least three influences. Culturally, there has been a growing mistrust of forms and of the authority they appear to represent. In psychological theory, Freud and his followers linked ritual to obsessional neuroses—although ritualized practices were and are clearly visible in many aspects of psychoanalytically-oriented treatment. In religious practice, in pastoral care theory, and especially in Clinical Pastoral Education, there has grown up an insistence that ritual ignores the particular in favor of the general, and that the use of rituals permits ministers to avoid dealing with difficult interpersonal situations.

---

[1] John T. McNeill's monumental *History of the Cure of Souls* (New York, NY: Harper, 1951) makes the shift from the personal to the formal in pastoral care very clear. But the shift from personal to formal did not originate with Christianity. In Judaism, a *b'rocha* is prescribed for many different specific situations, usually in a ritualized form: "Blessed art thou, O LORD God, King of the Universe, who..."

In the Presbyterian seminary I attended, pastoral care was taught as a series of formalized behaviors. In Situation A the pastor should engage in Activity A₁, in Situation B use B₁, and so on through the catalogue of human crises. I saw only a few years later that the forms—pastoral care rituals, worship rituals, and even formal clerical clothing—so valued in the Department of Practical Theology at that seminary were avoided and even despised by those most deeply grounded in pastoral care and counseling.

Today specialists in pastoral care in fact present no consistent picture in terms of the use of ritual. At a recent conference among such specialists, I spoke with a pastoral counselor who rigorously refused to conduct worship in any church setting where one of his clients might be attending worship, and with another who used ritual both in church worship services and in her counseling practice.

Pastoral care specialists have been lax in examining the relationship between pastoral care and ritual in a disciplined way.[2] There is, however, a growing consciousness that pastoral care and church ritual are far more deeply related to each other than has been ordinarily assumed.

Paul W. Pruyser, the late psychologist of religion who for many years directed the Department of Education at the Menninger Foundation, was troubled by the disuse and misuse of ritual in church life. In an essay written for a 1969 *Festschrift* in honor of Seward Hiltner, Pruyser discussed one particular aspect of ritual—benedictions and blessings—in his typically pungent style:

> Over the years, in attending worship services, I had gradually become accustomed to ministers terminating their services with a rushed and hardly audible benediction, uttered on the way out from the back of the sanctuary where nobody could see them. And if the benediction was pronounced from the pulpit, audibly and visibly, the spectacle for the beholders was often little more than a slovenly gesture, consisting of only one arm, raised half-heartedly and only half-way up, against the force of gravity to which that poor limb would quickly succumb again. [This experience is evidence] that there has been a steady decay in

---

[2] A significant and exciting exception is Elaine Ramshaw's *Ritual and Pastoral Care* (Philadelphia, PA: Fortress, 1987).

Protestantism of once powerful and wholesome symbols, or . . . the
replacement of symbols by mere emblems.[3]

Pruyser saw, more clearly than many of his contemporaries, the
intimate, subtle relationship between pastoral care and ritual. In
tracing that relationship, our first task is to understand more clearly
the nature of ritual.

The Nature of Ritual

A ritual is:

an ordered or patterned sequence of interpersonal behavior,
often occurring in connection with a particular event or circumstance,
performed in the same (or a very similar) way each time it occurs,
sometimes embodying a reference to a historical event, and
symbolizing—pointing beyond itself to—a value or a belief commonly
held by the individuals or groups who perform it.

This definition encompasses a wide variety of religious and non-
religious behaviors, from the "Minnesota farewells" affectionately
lampooned by Garrison Keillor to the most formal religious cere-
monies. It includes the ways a particular family celebrates holidays,
birthdays, and anniversaries. It includes such sacramental gestures as
laying on of hands at an ordination or in the giving of a blessing,
joining the hands of a marrying couple, or breaking the bread at a
eucharistic celebration. It excludes certain behaviors which, though
sometimes called ritualistic, grow out of a particular person's need
for defense against unwelcome experiences *(e.g.,* the "ritualized"
counting or handwashing engaged in by people suffering from com-
pulsive disorders).

In church bodies with a strong liturgical consciousness, the
proper performance of ritual may be carefully defined and described
by the church, and great value may be placed on performing the
ritual properly. In other churches rituals are equally present, but
tend to be considered informal or even casual rather than formally
prescribed. Even such supposedly informal rituals tend to have considerable power, however, and those who develop them will often resist very vigorously any attempt to alter them. Those who deviate may
suffer unpleasant social consequences. Any group of people regu-

[3]Paul W. Pruyser, "The Master Hand: Psychological Notes on Pastoral Blessing,"
in William B. Oglesby (Ed.), *The New Shape of Pastoral Theology* (New York, NY:
Abingdon, 1969), p. 353.

larly interacting with each other tends to attach to rituals feelings that, to an outsider, seem far more intense than an objective evaluation would warrant. Anthropologist Edward T. Hall calls this formal behavior: behavior based on an apparent assumption that there is no other way to do things.[4]

Functions or Meanings of Ritual

Rituals provide at least three things felt by those who participate in them to be valuable:

1. They offer a sense of identity, of "we-ness," which cements the bonds among members of a particular group. People who can say of themselves that "we do things this way" have a means of saying who they are and what they hold in common. The traditions of families, the liturgies of churches, and the customs of nations and ethnic groups all serve this function.

2. Rituals offer to participants a sense of living in a regular, reliable, trustworthy world. The Christmas decorations are put away with the confidence that these same ornaments and wreaths will be used to decorate the house and the tree next year. (In many families the ornaments are put away on the same day each year, perhaps New Year's Day or Epiphany.)

3. Rituals in many cases symbolize a deeply felt reality, a truth about God or self or life. They take on a kind of life from that reality. Theologian Paul Tillich argued that rituals, like all symbols, participate in the reality of that which they symbolize, and die if the reality behind them dies.

The Formation of Rituals

Any piece of behavior which someone finds useful, valuable, or even merely pleasant may be "nominated" to become a ritual, but the process is not as conscious as the word *nominated* might suggest. At first, it may be repeated merely because it has been experienced as appropriate, meaningful, or simply gratifying. Through repetition, the behavior takes on power. Meanings are often added by accretion, collecting over the years. Rituals formed in this way often bypass conscious processes of formation, and (partly because the process is kept out of conscious awareness) take on considerable psychological

---

[4]Edward T. Hall, *The Silent Language* (New York, NY: Doubleday, 1959).

power. Here the meaning of ritual resembles the function of religion as C. G. Jung saw it: to allow people to be in touch with their inmost depths without being overwhelmed by them .

There are other processes of formation: it is possible to invent a ritual, consciously to seek ways of symbolizing a felt reality. Rapid changes in a society and its patterns of relationship may prompt people to create rituals that express, or help to manage, feelings arising in reaction to the changes. Such conscious inventions are attempts to perform a function which simply accrues or develops in a less intentional process.

In the mid-1970s a committee of The United Methodist Church wrestled with issues of change and produced a book called *Ritual in a New Day: An Invitation.*[5] It included rituals for the dying, for the ending of marriages, and for other beginnings and endings. The strength of the book lay in its approach to previously uncharted areas; its weakness lay in its wordiness. It is characteristic that many consciously invented rituals, including those in the Methodist book, place heavy reliance on the spoken word. Other behaviors are not entirely omitted; one divorce ritual includes removing a wedding ring from the divorcing woman's left hand and placing it on the ring finger of the right hand "reconsecrated to her freedom."[6] But the principal reliance is on words; and all too often, the carefully chosen words lack the rhetorical power which frequently seems to come with the words of a ritual that has gradually evolved.[7]

In some cases new conditions and changed circumstances have been well-served by the adaptation and application of an already existing ritual originally evolved for a somewhat different purpose. Such rituals tend to have the emotional power of the original, but they run the risk of making misstatements about the nature of the situation to which they are being applied. If a ritual has been used in one situation and is now applied to another, participants tend to re-

---

[5]Alternate Rituals Editorial Committee of the Board of Discipleship of the United Methodist Church, *Ritual in a New Day: An Invitation* (New York, NY: Abingdon, 1976).

[6]*Ibid.*, p. 92.

[7]The heavy reliance on words in consciously constructed ritual often narrows or forces the meaning of the ritual. It may, in effect, say, "This means this, nothing more and nothing less." In doing so, the constructors run the risk of robbing the ritual of some of its power, for power is increased when the ritual speaks to the unconscious, and when it is susceptible of more than one interpretation.

gard this new situation as a mere variant of the first, rather than as something new and different.

Rituals also take on a life of their own, in a process closely akin to what Gordon Allport called "functional autonomy." This may mean that the ritual in question becomes so far removed from its origins that many would call it dead. Long after a ritual has ceased to fulfill the third function cited earlier, it may still fulfill the first two functions. Perhaps one might say that even when theologically dead in Tillich's sense, a ritual may for a time remain alive psychologically.

Ritual and Pathology

Many psychotherapists tend to hold ritual of any kind in contempt. Much psychoanalytic thought has adopted Freud's old assertion that there is a profound connection between obsessional states of mind and religious ritual. Therapists of various persuasions have expressed suspicion of ritual, warning us to be wary of any behavior on our own part that we regularly repeat. They have a valid point; many ritual behaviors can be used as defenses.

At the same time, most therapies and therapists have developed rituals of their own, differing from locale to locale and from one theoretical approach to another. American psychoanalysts tend to avoid the "handshaking ritual" prevalent in our society, while those in Europe tend to shake hands formally with analysands at each session. The ritualistic aspects of analytic meeting rooms, with their "icons of the saints," have frequently been noticed. So has the highly stylized language that therapists tend to use to identify members of their own "clubs." In one center where family systems theory is dominant, the use of the word *transference* is ritualistically avoided.

Psychotherapists often use ritual settings, ritualized language, and even ritualized postures and body movements—largely to keep anxiety at a minimum.

Ritual is not in itself antitherapeutic. Using it unconsciously, however, using it without knowing why one is using it, or using it as a means of exercising power and control, can all be antitherapeutic. Therapists' clients will often ascribe some kind of power to any ritualized behavior, and it is quite possible for a therapist to use rituals of some kind to take the edge off the therapist's own feelings of powerlessness or insecurity, at some cost to the client.

It is clear that some uses of ritual have a pathological basis. Rituals do in some ways serve as defenses against unwanted experience. Defenses, however, are not in themselves pathological, and often serve quite positive purposes. Pathology enters when defenses are misused or overused.

Pastoral Care Aspects of Liturgy

Many aspects of familiar liturgies have particular meaning for pastoral care. Specialists tend to be more interested in the way ritual may be used in pastoral care and counseling, but an approach "from the other direction" may be more important to parish pastors.

Liturgy in General. Calls to worship, assurances of pardon or absolution, benedictions, and other common elements in a worship service are likely to evoke a deep response from worshipers even when they are not consciously aware of it. Not long ago a member of a congregation returned to Sunday morning worship after having been hospitalized for a major heart attack. After the service she said to the minister: "The opening hymn was wonderful! Everybody sang so enthusiastically, and I felt like I could really lift up my heart and rejoice." The minister properly understood her comment to mean that pastoral care had been extended to this woman through the choice and singing of the hymn.

Among the great figures of the past half-century in pastoral care and counseling, Seward Hiltner was for many years the principal articulator of contemporary pastoral theology. One of his legacies— perhaps his greatest—is his perspectival approach, which affirms that there is no such thing as an instance of pastoral work that has only one meaning.[8] All pastoral care among Christians involves, however subtly, a proclamation of the Gospel; pastoral care among Jews involves, however subtly, an exposition of Torah. What concerns us here is the way the "shepherding" perspective shows up in rituals primarily intended for some other purpose.[9]

---

[8]Seward Hiltner, *Preface to Pastoral Theology* (New York, NY: Abingdon, 1959).

[9]The word *shepherding* has been controversial ever since Hiltner decided to use it. Many resent the implications of stupidity or willingness to be part of a herd which they believe they see in this word. Hiltner's original choice was of course not predicated on those implications but upon biblical imagery and upon the caring, self-giving qualities long associated with such imagery. But the negative implications of the metaphor are undeniable.

Consider again Paul Pruyser's comments upon the way a benediction is delivered. Liturgical theology and pastoral theology are likely to come to similar conclusions about such gestures. In some churches one can see a benediction delivered with hands at waist height, palms turned upward. In the history of liturgical theology that gesture is a beseeching attitude, the posture used for a prayer of petition. It is quite different from the classical posture for blessing advocated by Pruyser, in which it is clear that the "blesser" is giving something to someone. From the point of view of liturgical theology, the petition gesture does not say that the leader is delivering a blessing. The pastoral theologian would probably conclude that the minister has rejected the idea of delivering a blessing in the first place. Contained in that shift is a profound reshaping of the understanding of the nature of ministry.

As William Willimon has pointed out,[10] every element of the worship service has some potential use as pastoral care. Sermons may grow out of particular pastoral concerns.[11] Pastoral prayers may come to grips with issues and feelings. Postures, gestures, and ways of handling sacraments may touch upon issues too deep for words.

Sacraments. For many Christians, the sacraments are the primary meeting place of ritual and pastoral care. Many sacraments are symbolic reenactments of some event in the life and ministry of Jesus.[12] Although words accompany, and to some extent give specific meanings to, sacramental acts, sacraments convey meanings "too deep for words." One act may "contain" a very wide variety of meanings simultaneously.

The Eucharist in particular speaks to people in countless different ways about a variety of ideas and themes central to their faith and their lives. Because it is primarily a congregational sacrament, it often conveys the idea of membership, incorporation in a community, which may be powerfully felt by persons temporarily isolated by

---

[10]See William Willimon, *Worship as Pastoral Care* (Nashville, TN: Abingdon Press, 1979).

[11]When psychologist Harry Levinson worked at the Menninger Foundation, he defined a pastoral sermon as one which adequately described a hurt, put a label on it, and suggested clearly what could be done about it. From a Christian perspective, one might alter that slightly to include what God has already done about it.

[12]I use the term sacrament also to include what in various denominations are otherwise called "sacramentals" or ''ordinances."

illness or other circumstances. Because its symbols are common food and drink, it usually conveys the idea of sustenance. Because, unlike baptism, it is repeatable, it is available to believers at a wide variety of times in life. To administer the Eucharist is thus often a powerful act of pastoral care (even while it is many other things, as well.)

A consideration of the pastoral care aspects of the sacraments includes the recognition that their use is not without risk. The use of the Eucharist with the sick must be very carefully planned and needs prior interpretation. Every hospital chaplain has seen hospitalized believers terrified at the appearance of a minister with the elements of communion—it has felt to them like an omen of impending death. An almost converse risk is that ritual may be interpreted by more naive congregants as an act of magic, with *automatic* saving power, as if God could be manipulated by it. Such an interpretation gravely undercuts its value as an aspect of pastoral care.

The Use of Ritual in Pastoral Care and Counseling

Pastoral counselors and counseling agencies surround their clients with rituals. The routines of the office, the waiting room setting, the patterned way of beginning an hour, and other such regularities all form rituals in which client and counselor alike participate. To be sure, such rituals are of a slightly different sort than those we have been discussing, but they convey similar meanings. In particular, the rituals used in a counseling office provide a sense of identity and regularity which may be reassuring or annoying to the client. (More often it is reassuring.)

When we approach the use of ritual in pastoral care and counseling, we are treading on more difficult ground. It may be useful to cite two concrete incidents, one in the context of pastoral counseling, the other of pastoral care.

The first took place in the context of a pastoral counseling center, where a counselor was working with a middle-aged client whom we shall call Eloise. In one session, the hour was almost over. Eloise, frightened about her immediate future, was talking about her fears. Part of the fear came from her own past and her unusual childhood; part of it came from real dangers she was facing. She got up to leave, reached the door, and turned to stare at the pastoral counselor with a particularly intense look. The counselor remembered how often

Eloise had spoken of her attachment to Zenna Henderson's "People" stories.

The client, whose relationship with her own congregation was conflicted, would have rejected a "churchy" ritual, although she was a woman of faith. The counselor touched her forehead, and, quoting a line of blessing from a Zenna Henderson story very familiar to Eloise, said: "Go under the Protection." Months later, as the work was terminating, the client asked the counselor if she remembered the moment, and the counselor said, "Yes." "That," said the client, "was what turned everything around. I knew then that I could make it."

The other story comes from a theological seminary where a professor of New Testament took a strong pastoral interest in his students. Birgit, a student in her mid-thirties, realized with dismay that her marriage was irretrievably lost. She secured a divorce, but for more than a year afterward went about her work in the classroom crippled by guilt. She undertook a summer quarter of Clinical Pastoral Education, but her supervisor reported similar "crippling" in that setting. When she returned to school, the professor provided pastoral care for her in several conversations. One day, after a conversation with his colleague in the pastoral care department, the professor decided to offer a ritualized form of care to Birgit. Student and instructor planned the brief ritual together, but the professor told her that he wanted to be free to handle some aspects of the event in his own way.

The professor, in alb and purple stole, stood with Birgit and a dozen of her friends in the seminary chapel. The group read a prayer of confession in unison, and the professor read an assurance of pardon. Then he handed her a canvas book bag, which she held open. Into the bag the professor and the friends dumped pictures, books, and other items connected with her marriage. Then they stood silently for a few moments as Birgit held the now very heavy bag.

Then one of Birgit's friends took one handle of the bag and shared the weight. Again they stood in that position for a few moments, and then the professor reached over and drew Birgit's wedding ring (which she had put on for the ritual) from her finger, and dropped it in the bag. Again, in silence, they held their positions.

Finally, in what to Birgit was a surprise, the professor brought out a large pair of garden shears and severed the handles of the bag. It dropped to the stone floor with a thud.

Birgit knelt, and the group gathered around in silence, laying their hands on her head. After a silence, the professor said, "Go in peace," and the group quietly left the chapel.

The difficulties did not disappear overnight, but Birgit later said that this ceremony had marked the beginning of her healing.

Several issues connected with the use of ritual in pastoral care and counseling are visible in these two stories. Whether what was done in either case was wise or valid will of course depend upon the point of view from which one starts. For example, a pastoral counselor working from a psychodynamic perspective will probably find the blessing given to Eloise a problem. What was the meaning of the client's intense stare? Is it not probable that her look was an expression of transference, that she wanted her counselor/mother to save her from her anxiety? That, of course, is quite possible.

The counselor saw it differently. Though not unaware of transference issues, she knew that Eloise saw her and knew her as a clergywoman of Eloise's own denomination. She had already preached and baptized a baby in a worship service where Eloise was in attendance. More than anything else, she saw her primary identity as that of pastor, and chose to function with the ascribed power of the pastoral role. A far more urgent question in the counselor's mind was whether Eloise could accept and integrate any blessing. In retrospect, it seemed clear that: the blessing and the "Protection" were used by the client to provide a firm "working place" from which to wrestle with a number of anxiety-provoking issues.

It is interesting to contrast the scene in the counselor's office with the one in the seminary chapel. The post-divorce ritual was an instance of pastoral care in ritualized form, extended in a group setting (involving the recipient's relevant community of faith), while the "Henderson blessing" took place in a pastoral counseling context and involved only counselor and client. Those are significant differences. Transference, though present in the teacher-student relationship, was not an issue or a problem in the ritual; and the professor's standing as a representative figure in a faith community was made even clearer by the invitation to other members of the faith community to be present.

A useful principle can be surmised from this discussion: in a pastoral care context, the minister is functioning as a figure representing a faith community, and members of the community may even be present. In a pastoral counseling context, the relationship is more personalized, and almost never are representatives from the community involved. This does not necessarily mean that a pastoral counselor should never use a ritual of some sort; but it is a caution against careless use that can easily be misinterpreted.

Prayer

The single most frequent question raised about ritual in pastoral care and counseling has to do with prayer. Typical is the instance of the client in a church-sponsored counseling center. She was a moderately active member of a congregation that called itself evangelical; the counselor was a minister in the same denomination but not connected with her particular congregation. After several months of satisfying work, she suddenly reported to the counselor that some of her friends were advising her to terminate work with him, because he was not praying with her at every counseling session.

Typical, too, is the story of the recently ordained minister who regularly prayed with everyone he visited in homes and hospitals. He was astounded when one of the elderly women he called on asked him *not* to pray with her, and was inclined to attribute the request to a supposed lack of religious conviction on her part, until she pointed out that the things he prayed about were seldom her real concerns.

These two true stories serve as a caution that *always* and *never* are dangerous words to use in any instance of pastoral care. Those who always pray or who never pray (aloud) run the risk that we always run when we substitute routines for thinking. Prayer in pastoral care situations needs to be based on the attitudes and needs of the parishioner.

That caution extends to the way in which prayer is offered. Nico ter Linden tells the story of an uneducated, deeply religious Catholic who on his death bed pleaded with his priest, "Cain't ya please stop prayin' out of book?"[13] But he also tells of one of his own Dutch Reformed parishioners who insisted that the Christmas Eve service was not complete unless the minister used the ancient Latin formula, *"Puer nobis natus est."* Ministry to particular individuals depends on the pastor's knowledge of those individuals' particularities.

In pastoral counseling, there are likely to be fewer situations in which prayer will seem appropriate, primarily because people struggling with difficult issues often have a tendency toward the use of prayer, either as a defense or as magic, to avoid facing difficult problems or to alter situations magically. The underlying principles are the same, however. Always praying or never praying are both loaded with dangers, and there is no substitute for being aware of, and thinking carefully about, the particularities of the individual one is working with.

We often long for rules which will tell us specifically, definitively, what we should and should not do. That longing is built, by the way, on the same dynamic foundations as the neurotic use of rituals of which psychoanalysts are so suspicious. No absolute rules can be offered. But we are now in a position to set down some general principles which can guide counselors and carers:

Any given ritual may have a meaning for the person who decides to use it differently from meanings held by other participants. Thus it is important that the participants make sure that their use of the ritual makes a similar kind of sense to all involved.

Rituals which involve only two people are likely to carry with them more dangers than those which involve other representatives of a community. Whenever a community puts in the hands of some representative person the authority to conduct particular rituals, that person will be seen as having some kind of power. Psychologically, this process is akin to the transference; sociologically, it involves what is called ascribed power. Situations involving transference or ascribed power always carry the possibility of misuse, a possibility which is diluted when more than two people are involved. This is particularly true of rituals involving body movement and/or touch.

---

[13]Nico ter Linden, *In the Lord's Boarding House* (Nashville, TN: Abingdon Press, 1985).

Nevertheless, the value of touch is very great, particularly in situations involving anything approximating a blessing. Praying with sick or grieving folk and offering them a blessing or a benediction ought whenever possible to involve touch. Pruyser writes: "Most pastors . . . do [this] almost instinctively, because they know 'in their bones' that tragic situations always call for some kind of touch, some kind of effortless self-giving, some direct, primitive, unreflected, spontaneous spilling over of affect into the motor system."[14]

Although rituals may be constructed for a specific situation, it is valuable to make use of already existing rituals whenever possible. Sometimes it isn't possible; no ritual exists for a given situation, or the ones that do are inadequate. But in general something that is done once to meet a specific need (a) is not a ritual in the first place, and (b) will probably be constructed with too little regard for principles underlying good use of words or of movement.

Conclusion

Pastoral care is deeply and powerfully associated with ritual, a fact that we are only recently beginning to recover. There exists— there has always existed— danger that rituals will be misused, but principles do exist for the guidance of pastors and counselors. Meanwhile, there are dangers even deeper in avoiding and neglecting this fundamental pastoral resource.

---

[14]In Oglesby, *The New Shape of Pastoral Theology,* p. 362.

Lay Pastoral Care

RONALD H. SUNDERLAND, Ed. D.,
Research Fellow, Institute of Religion, Texas Medical Center,
PO Box 20569, Houston, TX 77225

"You are a chosen race, a royal priesthood, a holy nation, God's own people, that you may declare the wonderful deeds of him who called you out of darkness into his marvellous light."
—I Peter 2:9 (NEB)

Thehe images in this biblical passage were addressed by Lesslie Newbigin in a conference of Australian churches held in 1960. Bearing in mind that the writer of the Epistle was addressing the whole church—the entire *laos*—Newbigin focussed on the image of a priesthood shared by all baptized people. He contended that the whole church is a royal priesthood, the place where the love of God is made available to people, and the forgiveness of God is mediated to people. The church in its whole being is to be "that fluorescent screen in which the invisible sovereignty of God over all things is made visible and credible, in which the wonderful deed of him who called you out of darkness into his marvellous light are manifested." He continued:

> This priestly ministry of the whole Church is to be carried out through its entire membership. The Christian (member) at his (or her) daily task is the bearer of it. Is it not an illusion that constantly fogs our thinking about the Church that we think of it as something that exists manifestly on Sunday, is in a kind of state of suspended animation from Monday to Saturday, and, unlike most animals, hibernates in summer? The truth of course is that the Church exists in its prime reality, from Monday to Saturday, in all its members, dispersed throughout fields and homes and offices and factories, bearing the royal priesthood of Christ into every corner of His world.[1]

---

[1] Lesslie Newbigin, "Four Talks on I Peter," *We Were Brought Together,* Report of the National Conference of Australian Churches, Melbourne, Australia, February 2-4, 1960 (Sydney: Australian Council of Churches, 1960) (See also Ronald H. Sunderland, "The Character of Servanthood," in Earl E. Shelp & Ronald H. Sunderland, (Eds.), *The Pastor as Servant* (New York, NY: The Pilgrim Press, 1986) .

The images used by Newbigin were repeated constantly in the 1950s and 1960s by such theologians as Yves Congar, Hans Ruedi-Weber, Stephen Neill, John A.T. Robinson, Colin Williams, Hendrik Kraemer, and Gibson Winter.[2] Much of what was written during those two decades was inspired by studies generated by the World Council of Churches (WCC) and its national affiliates. It was set in the context of the movement toward renewal of the congregation and the construction of paracongregational agencies. It was a favorite theme to stress the image that, for the growth of a spontaneously evangelistic church, there would need to be a rhythm of God's people "being gathered together for worship that consists of praise, and being scattered and sent out into the world for worship that consists of obedience." [3]

Pastoral Care as Lay Ministry

Such were the ringing phrases of the mid years of the century. But there was missing from the spate of materials emanating from the WCC's Department of the Laity and the Division of World Mission and Evangelism any reference to the church's *pastoral* ministry as a vehicle for its service in the world. Without exception, the emphasis was on the responsibility of laypeople to witness to the power of the gospel, with special reference to accomplishing the task in the workplace. A great deal was said about the layperson's daily job as a Christian vocation. It was suggested, for example, that the social activities of men and women need the impact of the love of Christ, but the church was too often concerned only to seek the redemption of an individual soul, without reference to the individual's environment. Laypeople were being called to be servants of God within the structures of the secular world. Theologians were anxious that old images of "extraction evangelism" must be replaced by

---

[2]Yves Congar, *Lay People in the Church* (London: Chapman, 1959); Hans Ruedi-Weber, *Signs of Renewal* (Geneva: World Council of Churches, 1957); John A.T. Robinson, *Layman's Church* (London: Lutterworth, 1963); also *The New Reformation* (London: SCM Press, 1965); Colin Williams, *Where in the World* (New York, NY: National Council of Churches, 1963), also, *What in the World* (New York, NY: National Council of Churches, 1964); Hendrik Kraemer, *A Theology of the Laity* (Philadelphia, PA: Westminster Press, 1958); Gibson Winter, *The Suburban Captivity of the Churches* (New York, NY: Doubleday & Company, 1961).

[3]Hans Ruedi-Weber, "The Local Congregation in the Evangelistic Task of the Churches," *We Were Brought Together*, Report of the National Council of Australian Churches, Melbourne, Australia, February 2-11, 1960 (Sydney: Australian Council of Churches, 1960), p. 88.

newer forms of proclaiming the gospel, but it was not immediately clear just *how* this task was to be performed.

Perhaps the reason for the fact that pastoral care as lay ministry was overlooked was that since the 1950s emphasis on the development of clinical pastoral training had remained the province of a small group of theologians and clinicians in the United States whose work failed to make any impact on the larger question of the nature and mission of the church. In part, it may have occurred because, while questions of ecclesiology were focusing on the relationship of clergy and lay ministries, matters of pastoral ministry remained the province of the clergy. To put it in the simplest terms possible, clergy were educated to provide the congregation's *pastoral* ministry, while laypeople were expected to witness to their faith in "the world" ; that is, to be responsible for the church's evangelism efforts. Alan Richardson, however, was speaking for many of his contemporaries when he stated that the early church regarded baptism as ordination to the ministry of the church:

> There are no "lay" members of the Church who are without a ministry in it; the Church is a ministerial priesthood of the laity of people of God. We must not allow the development of a special order of *deakonai* to obscure the truth that the whole community and every individual member of it were a ministry which participated in the one ministry of Christ.[4]

It does not seem to have been apparent to the forefathers and mothers of the Clinical Pastoral Education movement that what was being said concerning renewal and the role of the laity applied to the specific areas in which the church's pastoral ministry was set. Hans Ruedi-Weber had written, for example, that "the laity are not the helpers of the clergy so that the clergy can do their jobs, but the clergy are the helpers of the whole people of God so that the laity can be the Church."[5] But in the ministry of pastoral care, the ordained minister remained the functionary.

---

[4]Alan Richardson, *An Introduction to the Theology of the New Testament* (New York, NY: Harper and Brothers, 1958), p. 304.

[5]Hans Ruedi-Weber, as quoted by John A.T. Robinson, *Layman's Church* (London: Lutterworth Press, 1963), p. 17.

The Pastoral Theology "Fathers"

In his presentation of his basic assumptions of pastoral counseling in 1949, Seward Hiltner had written only of the role of the ordained minister. This was doubtless for two reasons. First, in 1949 the tide was only just beginning to turn in the direction of renewal and rediscovery of the role of laypeople in the church. Secondly, and more important, clinical pastoral training was still on the defensive, and the place for its contribution to theological education still had to be defended. This Hiltner did in his book, asserting that theological students needed to be in contact with people in the clinical setting of the general or mental hospital. Here "conditions were best designed to teach him how to help them as a minister." [6] Hiltner could still refer to the early days of clinical training as only being fifteen years earlier. The work of pioneering was still going on, and it could not have occurred to its exponents to extend pastoral training beyond the professional clergy. Moreover, this function of the clergy clearly involved them in the sphere of interest of the other healing professions. Any suggestion that " non-professionals " should participate in this work may have seriously alienated these helping professions on the support and assistance of which Clinical Pastoral Education has leaned so heavily. Another reason for the restriction of attention to the work of the clergy may have been that the pastoral theologians used the terms "pastoral care" and "pastoral counseling" very loosely. Since either function was virtually restricted to the clergy, it may be that this was not noticed; if pastoral counseling was merely an extension of the ordained pastor's role, the lack of precision may have seemed unimportant.

Writers in the field of pastoral care who directed their attention solely to the work of the ordained minister drew heavily on the "shepherd" image as a symbol for the minister, with the consequent limitations of that image noted by Wise and others. Nevertheless, Hiltner laid a tentative foundation for the later extension of the ministry of pastoral counseling beyond that of the ordained minister to the lay membership of the church. He stated that "Counseling is an activity, not a profession . . ., a process of relationship between one who seeks and one who gives help, carried out in a more or less prominent, more or less time-consuming aspect of the professional

---

[6] Seward Hiltner, *Pastoral Counseling* (Nashville, TN: Abingdon Press, 1949), pp. 66-71; also pp. 243-46.

activities of the helper."[7] It is true that Hiltner implies a professional stance, but this is qualified, and there is no inherent reason, given the same pre-requisites as would apply to ordained clergy—adequate training *and* supervision—why selected laypeople should not share in this aspect of the church's work.

Hiltner moved further in the direction of lay involvement in pastoral care in *Preface to Pastoral Counseling*, published in 1958, in which he developed the concept of pastoral care as "shepherding." This is offered as a "perspective" rather than a definitive and exclusive stereotype. He proposed that the model of shepherding suggests an identification with pastoral care, as long as the latter "is seen to be involved in some degree in every act of church and minister, and to be dominantly important in some acts but not in others."[8] This was extended to include laypeople, a transition that Hiltner believed had not been previously made. "The discussion of the person in pastoral theology has so far concentrated on ministers as ordained clergymen who have had theological education." He asks: "Is pastoral theology a concern only of the clergy? Is there not a universal pastorhood to go along with the universal priesthood of Protestantism?"[9] Clearly, the prerequisite is not a professional role, but appropriate training and supervision. Given the prevailing preoccupation with clergy-dominated ministry, Hiltner was understandably cautious with the areas of pastoral care in which he saw the possibility of lay involvement, but a start had been made. He clearly was addressing the emerging discipline of pastoral *counseling*, however, and it should be understood that "lay pastoral *care*" excludes the function of counseling unless the lay minister has undertaken appropriate training and is functioning under professional supervision.

Other writers, however, began to turn attention to the general field of pastoral care in the congregation as an appropriate ministry for laypeople. Daniel Day Williams derived the authority of the church's ministry from the authority of Christ, who brought the church into being.[10] The servant nature of this ministry was clearly stated, with the implication that what is being discussed is the min-

---

[7]*Ibid.*, p. 95.

[8]Seward Hiltner, *Preface to Pastoral Counseling* (New York, NY: Abingdon Press, 1958), p. 19.

[9] *Ibid.*, pp. 37-38. See also William B. Oglesby, Jr., "Lay Pastoral Care Revisited," *The Journal of Pastoral Care*, 1986, Vol. 40, No. 2, pp. 119-128.

istry of the *church,* not that which is limited to a select group; that is, the clergy. Nevertheless, without explanation, Williams treated the pastoral function of the ordained minister as if it bore no relation to the ministry of the congregation, leaving one to assume that this is at best a vicarious ministry in which the minister acts on behalf of the members.

In 1964, Wayne Oates[11] suggested that the demands on the clergy to provide pastoral care would become overwhelming. This should lead clergy to gather into groups those around them who needed help, so enabling clergy to use their time more effectively. When choosing leaders for classes in the teaching ministry of the congregation, reference is made to the need for maturity on the part of the leaders, who will be engaged in meeting many inner needs of people. Further than that, Oates did not go. Two years later, Carroll Wise wrote *The Meaning of Pastoral Care.* Throughout this book, he did not depart from the emphasis which he established in his opening paragraph, where he stated that "the living model of pastoral care *for the ordained minister* (emphasis added) is the person and work of Jesus Christ." He added: "A Christian pastor is one who in his person and in his living relationships with people mediates something of the quality of being which is found in a large measure in the revelation of Christ."[12]

Wise then questioned the adequacy of the "shepherd" image for the minister, and in its place urged his readers to draw on a more meaningful and powerful symbol; namely, that which Paul uses in II Cor. 5, with its stress on the experience of reconciliation. He pointed to a second Pauline passage, I Cor. 12 :4-13 :13 . In neither case did he depart from the assumption of his introductory pages; that is, that the primary figure in the church's ministry of pastoral care is the ordained minister. Yet in both instances, Paul is addressing the whole church, not a select group within the church. It is not only the pastor who is called to the ministry of reconciliation, but every minister, lay and ordained. The exclusive aspect of Wise's concept of pastoral care was further emphasized later on when he writes that "pastoral

---

[10]Daniel D . Williams, *The Minister and the Care of Souls (New York, NY:* Harper and Brothers, 1961).

[11]Wayne E. Oates, *The Christian Pastor* (Philadelphia, PA: Harper and Row, 1964), p. 34, also p. 36.

[12]Carroll Wise, *The Meaning of Pastoral Care* (New York, NY: Harper and Row, 1966), p. 1.

care is the manifestation in the relationship between *pastors* and persons . . . of a quality of love which points to, and gives a basis for, the realization of the love of God." Again:

> Pastoral experience, as well as the Gospel itself, clearly indicates the necessity of the mutual involvement of *pastor* and person. In this involvement the pastor is not just another person— a father, a mother, a friend—but is one whose involvement demonstrates and gives substance to the message of God's grace.[13]

Even when Wise described pastoral care as the mediation of God's grace to another person, he did so in terms of its manifestation in the pastoral acts of the ordained minister: the pastor is placed "in a living relationship with God and man, that is, he is to love those whom he serves just as God in Christ has loved both him and them."

He continued immediately:

> We would not confine this level of communication to the pastor. It is also the responsibility of the layman. But we are saying that it is this dimension which distinguishes *real* pastoral care from *mere pastoral activity*. The pastor should have a level of training and wisdom in such matters beyond that which most laymen are not *(sic)* privileged to acquire.[14] (emphasis added)

It is certainly true that the pastor should have a level of training beyond that which most laypeople *are* privileged to acquire. It is, however, very difficult to find a New Testament justification for a concept of the church which distinguishes between the ministry of the ordained minister and that of laypeople solely on the basis of training. The implication is that the pastor exercises pastoral care, while laypeople, being untrained, engage in "mere pastoral activity." As to the proposal that clergy should have a monopoly of wisdom in such matters, *that* is impossible to justify, either biblically or experientially. Even when Wise enumerated the "fruits of the spirit," this was offered solely with reference to their expression in the life of the pastor, though the New Testament proposes that these gifts are granted to the whole fellowship. The problem with which Wise's reader was confronted was that, while lip service was given to the conviction that pastoral care was the responsibility of the congrega-

---

[13] *Ibid*., pp . 13-14.
[14] *Ibid.*, p. 26.

tion, it was the ordained minister to whom the concept was addressed.

The Broadening of the Concept

By the mid-sixties, there was evidence that the stereotype was being questioned. Howard Clinebell chartered ways in which the congregation may become a center of healing and growth, citing many avenues in which laypeople may participate in this work. He referred to "current experimentation in the pastoral care ministry of the laity as an encouraging sign."[15] In a chapter entitled "The Layman's Ministry of Pastoral Care and Counseling," he stressed that the implications of the lay renaissance for pastoral care were profound. He referred to a number of congregational projects which illustrated Hiltner's image of the "pastorhood of all believers."

One of the most forceful statements was made by C.W. Brister in *Pastoral Care in the Church*. He listed the emergence of a responsible pastoral theology based on a new understanding of pastoral care, the renaissance of biblical study, the ecumenical conversation within the church, and the laity's role in the mission of the church as four of the most crucial movements in the contemporary (American Protestant) scene. He addressed himself to the broad question: "What is pastoral care?" He placed the emphasis on pastoral care as a ministry of the church:

> Protestant pastoral care views the Church itself as minister, and the pastor as a servant of servants. His role as leader, teacher and example is fulfilled within the Church's shepherding ministry. God's people care for hurt humanity as they incarnate His redemptive presence in life, where the real needs are (John 17:15-26). The Church thus finds its life in the world by grappling with the evils, distress, and unanswered questions of men "for Christ's sake."[16]

Brister suggested that two steps were necessary to provide for a pastoral ministry shared by clergy and laypeople. First, the minister must train the laypeople for their task. Second, "today's agents of reconciliation must shape their service to people's needs where they are; the Samaritan ministered to a neighbor as he travelled on the

---

[15]Howard J. Clinebell, *Basic Types of Pastoral Counseling* (Nashville, TN: Abingdon Press, 1966), p. 16.

[16]C.W. Brister, *Pastoral Care in the Church* (New York, NY: Harper and Row, 1964), p. xxiii.

open road."[17] At this, as at other crucial points, Brister substantiated his thesis by reference to biblical sources, and by consistently returning to amplify his dominant motif that the church's shepherding ministry to the world is the corporate responsibility of *pastor and people alike.*

Consciously or unconsciously, Brister had built a bridge between the theologians of the 1950s and 1960s who addressed issues of church and congregational renewal, and the Clinical Pastoral Education movement, which had developed the expertise and experience by which laypeople could be equipped to express gifts of ministry through the congregation's pastoral care activity. But the victory was not won without a rear-guard action. Not all theologians were convinced that laypeople had a rightful place in pastoral care. William Clebsch and Charles Jaekle had raised the same question addressed by Brister: What is the content of pastoral care by which one action is deemed a pastoral act of the church, while another is excluded from this category? They spoke of a "plethora of helpful acts" which are closely related to pastoral care, but do not belong to that specific ministry. "On many occasions, works of charity, of welfare, of education, of the binding up of wounds, of giving ethical counsel, and so forth, have come to be closely associated with the Christian ideal of love for the neighbor."[18] They stated that if there was lacking from this generous activity "any special representation of Christian faith to troubles eliciting ultimate concerns," such helping acts, however admirable, are hardly pastoral. Pastoral care, they argued, is not synonymous with acts of mercy, or with works of love and charity, or with neighborliness! Unless the Name was named, it was not pastoral ministry!

The matter of the relationship between speech and act had been raised by Karl Barth.[19] In addition to the questions Barth raised, other questions are implicit: Is Christian witness as speech invested with greater priority, or importance, than the act which accompanies it, or, sometimes, stands in its stead? Is it possible to exercise a Christian presence by being in a situation in the name of Christ without being identified by "word"? Matthew 25 seems to indi-

---

[17]*Ibid., p.* 85.

[18] William A. Clebsch and Charles R. Jaekle, *Pastoral Care in Historical Perspective* (Englewood Cliffs, NJ: Prentice Hall, 1964), p. 7.

[19]Karl Barth, *Church Dogmatics* (Edinburgh: T. & T. Clark, 1962), IV/3, p. 863 ff.; also 1/1, pp. 55, 61ff., 162 ff..

cate the possibility. Schubert Ogden comments on the passage, suggesting that what is indispensable is what that passage says is indispensable. "The striking note sounded by the parable is that, on Judgment Day, we will apparently not be asked whether we believe in God. We will be asked how we acted in the face of the immediate needs of our neighbors. And we should expect that what holds good on Judgment Day is expected of us here and now."[20]

Pastoral Care as Christian Presence

The term, "Ministry of Presence," has been popularized of late to draw attention to the relational character of pastoral care. William 0. Avery drew attention to the frequency with which students returning to the seminary from CPE centers used the term to amplify their perceptions of pastoral ministry. They had discovered that "their 'presence' is often more important than their words."[21]

The term "Christian presence" is used as an expression of the sense of I Peter 2:9 that we are called to proclaim the wonderful deeds of him who calls us out of darkness into his marvelous light. The term was used first by the French worker-priests shortly after the Second World War. It was adopted by the World Student Christian Federation (W.S.C.F.) for a conference held in the Netherlands in 1964, when it came to my attention. In the conference report, the participants spoke of their effort to understand the particular ministry to which they were called in the academic world. How were they to exercise a Christian presence in the academic community?

The report spoke of taking one's place in the world in the name of Christ, often anonymously, hoping that others will recognize Jesus for who he is and stay where they are,

> involved in the fierce fight against all that dehumanizes, ready to act against demonic powers, to identify with the outcase, merciless in ridiculing new idols and new myths. When we say "presence," we say that we have to get into the midst of things even when they frighten us.

---

[20]Schubert Ogden, personal communication, as quoted by Ronald H. Sunderland, "The Character of Servanthood," in Earl E. Shelp & Ronald H. Sunderland (Eds.), *The Pastor as Servant* (New York, NY: The Pilgrim Press, 1986), pp. 43-44.

[21]William 0. Avery, "Toward an Understanding of the Ministry of Presence," *The Journal of Pastoral Care*, 1986, Vol. 40, No. 4, p. 343.

Once we are there, we may witness fearlessly to Christ, if the occasion is given; we may also have to be silent.[22]

I use this passage to suggest guidelines to laypeople who have acknowledged the congregation's call to train and serve in the ministry of pastoral care. When one is sensitive to the cries of people for support and help—for pastoral care—one may be present to such a person, expecting that the form that care will take will become known in that situation. What does become clear very quickly is that in such situations the caring person does have options that include letting one's presence in service speak for itself, while being open to the possibility of "naming the Name," in some formal sense of witness.

The W.S.C.F. conference statement continued:

Presence for us means engagement, involvement in the concrete structures of our society. It indicates a priority. First, we have to be there before we can see our task clearly. In one sense of the word, presence precedes witness. In another sense, the very presence is witness.[23]

This interrelationship between "word" and "act" is one not of contrast but of interdependence. Laypeople need to be free to move comfortably from one to the other as the occasion for ministry suggests. For those laypeople whose gifts lie in the area of the congregation's pastoral care ministry, the act of ministering may be the mode in which the gospel takes shape in their lives and in those of others.

A Presbyterian elder told how she had returned to the supermarket to pick up a few items she had forgotten earlier. As she stood in the express register line and glanced around, she became aware that the face of the register clerk appeared strained. As she watched, she sensed the woman was in shock and obviously finding it difficult to function. Yet the customers ahead of her were paying for their items and leaving without any apparent attention to the clerk. As she drew level with the clerk, the elder asked the woman if she was all right, adding, "You look as if you are in distress." The clerk paused and responded: "I don't know how you can tell, but I have never

---

[22]"The Christian Community in the Academic World," Report of the World Student Christian Federation General Committee, July, 1964. *Student World*, 1965, No. 3, p. 234.

[23]*Ibid.*, p. 234.

been in a situation like this in my life. I have never been treated like this before. I don't think I can go on." With these words, the clerk slumped against the register. The elder looked around, and noting the line of new customers behind her, saw that this was neither the time nor the place for an extended pastoral conversation. She turned back to the clerk and said: "I am sorry that you are hurting. I just want you to know I care." The clerk looked up in surprise and replied: "You are the first person who has said anything like that to me. I think I can manage on that."

As the lay elder later reflected on her "ministry" with other members of her congregation's pastoral ministry team, she linked her own experience of God's grace with the words she had said, sharing with her fellow ministers that she just found the words on her lips! "I could not ignore the clerk's pain. There was something I needed to say. I knew I was there in the name of Christ." She added, "but it did not seem appropriate to add that." I propose that, contrary to the argument advanced by Clebsch and Jaekle, this was pastoral ministry, offered self-consciously in the name of Christ in a situation which called for a pastoral response. That is, it was the elder's identity as a lay minister that made the conversation "pastoral."

Equipping Laypeople for Ministry

In November, 1973, I was invited by a local pastor to assist him to train a group of elders for the congregation's pastoral ministry. I responded that I had had no experience in this field; my work had been restricted to Clinical Pastoral Education in which clergy and seminary students functioned full-time in a hospital setting. Nevertheless, I was committed to the concept, and when the pastor suggested that the time was ripe to enlarge my experience, I did not need a second request. My experience informed me that one could not equip laypeople for pastoral care by lecturing. But, I assumed, they did not have any clinical experience on which I could base didactic sessions. I therefore selected two verbatim reports of pastoral visits in the hospital which had been written by two of my current group of students, one a seminary student, the second an ordained minister. Both sessions proved that my judgment was in error. The group members informed me they could not learn from such material; they would not make visits like those, they added. When asked how they would have approached either visit, they could not provide an answer; they only knew they would not have ministered like the two CPE students had attempted to minister. I abandoned this teaching method and, in the third sessions, delivered a lecture on "Death and Dying!" By then, I had exhausted my own ideas. The pastor then proposed to ask each trainee to make a pastoral visit in the congregation prior to the fourth session, which we would use to review their work. I protested that they had not yet learned how to visit. Yet the idea was inescapable. The laypeople made their visits and we reviewed them. If I was unready then for the experience of surprise at the quality of most of their visits, I have long since moved beyond surprise, and have come to expect as a normal occurrence the high quality and effectiveness of the pastoral care offered by trained laypeople.

Out of this initial experience, a training method did in fact emerge. Following a limited training period, laypeople are assigned to make pastoral calls on church families. They write verbatims, and are supervised in groups, with individual oversight when indicated. The training program best suited to equipping laypeople includes:

1. Reading and reviewing pastoral visits made by laypeople. This process introduced them to the form and directions lay visits may take.

2. Introduction of the concept of "story-listening." Much, if not all, lay pastoral care consists properly of listening to the member's story of hardship, anxiety, grief, hurt, or of celebration and achievement. (One of the tragedies of a model of pastoral care restricted to clergy is that the congregation's pastoral ministry is reduced to crisis response—and not even all those visits can be fitted into the pastor's busy schedule! Too often, occasions for personal or family celebrations are overlooked as occasions for pastoral visits).

3. The story-listening concept is applied to the traditional areas of congregational care: hospital, bereavement and home-bound ministries.

4. Attention is given to recognizing the lay minister's own personal needs, emotions, and limits, which will, if unrecognized, intrude upon the pastoral relationship.

5. The function of pastoral care is related to the wider ministry of the congregation and, in particular, to the work of evangelism.

6. With the completion of the initial training sessions, members of the team are invited to review their experience of training, and to assess their sense of call to ministry in a setting in which designated representatives of the congregation provide feedback on their review of

each participant's readiness for ministry. At the conclusion of this process, those laypeople to be called to the congregation's ministry are presented to the congregation and commissioned for their task.

The Scope of Lay Pastoral Care

There are few, if any, areas of pastoral care in which laypeople are inherently unable to minister. The only significant exclusion is indicated by the theology of sacramental ministry by which a particular faith community shapes its life. Even in this area, the practice of ministry is changing. The model of lay eucharistic ministry adopted by the Catholic church is now being replicated in some Episcopal church dioceses. In such settings, a commissioned lay ministry offers pastoral care in the setting of the eucharistic celebration—for one cannot bring the Eucharist to Mr. and Mrs. Johnson without that celebration becoming the occasion for a pastoral visit. Laypeople are able to function effectively in hospital, bereavement, and home-bound settings, representing the congregation's pastoral care ministry. In fifteen years of working with groups of lay pastoral ministers, I am continually awestruck, not by the fact that laypeople do minister, but by the depth and sensitivity of their expressions of care. As a clinical pastoral supervisor, it is salutary to recognize that laypeople gifted with the *charism* of pastoral care can minister as effectively as clergy, and often with greater effectiveness.

One of the objections which is most often met is that congregants will not accept laypeople as pastoral ministers, demanding instead a visit from the "real" minister; that is, the senior pastor. The overwhelming weight of evidence indicates that perception of effective pastoral care by the church member depends on the quality of the care received, not on the identity of the care-giver. A visit by a younger laywoman to a 65 year-old member began with the member's retort: "Well, why are you here? Why didn't he come himself? Why did he have to send someone else?" Forty minutes later, at the close of the visit during which, judged by any standard, effective caring ministry had been offered and received, the lay visitor asked if she might pay a further visit. The member responded: "Yes, please come back, a visit means a lot to me."

The concept of lay pastoral care must now be enlarged to include not only the customary forms of pastoral ministry, but what has traditionally been regarded as "evangelism" visits. "Pastoral Care" includes *any* pastoral contact between the congregation and one of its families or members. Many clergy are aware that appointment to the Evangelism Committee of the congregation is met with greater resistance than is evoked by other tasks. That task is perceived as less onerous when the visit is viewed as a pastoral visit (in the sense proposed in previously under the heading, "Pastoral Care as Christian Presence"). If the purpose of a visit to a church member or family is construed as an opportunity to make the acquaintance of the family with a view to strengthening the pastoral relationship with the individual or family, and to express the care of the congregation for the family in the broadest terms, neither the visitor nor the family member(s) feel threatened, judged, or under pressure to perform in certain ways. Thus, for example, ministry to inactive families, to people who have attended worship services or other congregational activities as visitors, or welcome calls on new families arriving in the neighborhood are properly seen as aspects of the pastoral activities of the congregation. Training for these ministries becomes part of the pastoral education program.

Oversight—the Key to Effective Ministry

Robert Burns observed that "the best laid schemes o' mice an' men gang aft a-gley." That is certainly manifested in the history of both evangelism projects and, more recently, lay pastoral care efforts. The primary reason for the failure of many evangelism projects and lay pastoral care ministries in congregations has been the reluctance or inability of clergy to initiate rigorous supervision of lay ministers. The best training methods and materials available will represent wasted efforts—and money—if continuing, consistent oversight is not introduced at the outset. Much of the church's investment in elaborate evangelism projects has been frittered away because the initial training was not reinforced by adequate oversight.

Supervision will normally take the form of what Clinical Pastoral Education knows as the "verbatim seminar." Pastoral visitors write a verbatim record of their conversation and present the account of the visit to a group session convened by a pastoral supervisor. When issues of confidentiality or other aspects of a visit indicate, a pastoral conversation may be supervised on a one-to-one basis with the supervisor. This process of supervision, or oversight, of pastoral ministry is at the heart of the genius of Clinical Pastoral Education. For sixty years the clinical process has been developed, investigated, and strengthened by the Association for Clinical Pastoral Education and its predecessors. The result is a finely tuned process that is highly effective in educating clergy, seminarians and, more recently, laypeople, for the church's pastoral care ministry. It is a small step to translate this educational process into the life of the congregation. The supervisory group provides support to the pastoral team members, an opportunity for continuing education in ministry and, at its heart, pastoral care of the pastoral carers. Indeed, it is important to recognize that the equipping of people, whether lay or clergy, for ministry does not happen in the classroom but in regular reflection on day-to-day ministry. At best, a training program can stimulate interest in ministry and orient the participant to specific functions of care. But the CPE movement has demonstrated conclusively that the action-reflection model which provides for continuing oversight is a necessary condition for effective functioning.

There is, however, a catch. The process assumes the availability of competent supervisors. When the Intern Program was being developed by Perkins School of Theology, I found that some clergy intuitively grasped the elements of the supervisory process, and provided effective oversight of the seminary interns. Other clergy had not previously utilized supervisory skills or concepts and, without training, were ineffective. Assuming a rigorous selection process, we found that clergy not previously oriented to supervision could acquire those skills and provide effective oversight. Moreover, while the supervisory training process of the ACPE requires an elaborate and intensive two-year commitment, we found that clergy could provide competent oversight of seminarians with brief, short-term training *provided* that they submitted to the on-going oversight of the Perkins' staff. We have demonstrated that this phenomenon holds good for equipping laypeople for ministry. Pastors do not emerge from seminary with supervisory skills. Indeed, few graduate with the expectation of equipping and supervising laypeople in ministry. But these skills can be acquired, leading to the initiation of effective lay pastoral ministry in their congregations.

When I began to implement this concept, I was often challenged by lay participants concerning my emphasis on supervision by clergy. May not laypeople become effective supervisors? The answer is a qualified "Yes." Many laypeople, by virtue of their own professional training, may already possess supervisory skills far beyond those that many clergy have acquired. Other laypeople, while not possessing formal skills, nevertheless may use their intuitive grasp of the concept to offer significant oversight. The functions being supervised, however, are *pastoral* in nature. Reflection on pastoral care will usually require theological expertise; that is, the close involvement of the ordained pastor. Development of lay pastoral care programs thus provides clergy with a setting in which to draw on their resources of pastoral and theological identity in ways which give new meaning to their ordination and ministry. Perhaps this is what the writer to the Ephesians had in mind when declaring the Holy Spirit gives gifts, "some to be apostles, some prophets, some evangelists, some pastors and teachers, to equip God's people for work in his service" (Ephes. 4:12; NEB). The ordained minister who trains laypeople to share with him or her in the congregation's pastoral ministry finds new opportunities to serve them as pastor, as their "theologian in residence," and as their teacher and fellow-member of the household of faith.

In summary, I hold that pastoral care is one of the tasks for which members of the congregation are "gifted," and, therefore, should be called upon to fulfill. Lay ministry should be accountable to the congregation and, therefore, should be subject to oversight. Such supervision will usually fall to the ordained minister, and the development of the Clinical Pastoral Education movement has created in the church a source of expertise to train clergy for this function.

Postscript

It seems logical to suggest that supervisory training should be initiated in the seminary so that candidates for ordination and appointment to their first parishes would approach that point committed to and prepared for their function as equippers of laypeople for pastoral ministry. Students having received an introduction to supervision prior to graduation, the seminary could continue its service to clergy through a continuing education program which consolidates their learning by supervising their oversight of lay ministry. For its part, the clinical pastoral education movement is faced with an unequalled opportunity to capitalize on its remarkable source of knowledge and clinical skills, thus fulfilling its servant role within the church.

Pastoral Care of the Elderly

MELVIN A. KIMBLE, Ph.D.,
Professor of Pastoral Theology and Ministry,
Luther Northwestern Theological Seminary,
St. Paul, MN 55108

More than half of the average clergy's clinical pastoral work, David Moberg hypothesizes, is directly related to aging.[1] These pastoral care tasks are diverse and challenging for there is no population that is more heterogeneous than the elderly.

Knowledge about aging is a prerequisite for effective and responsible pastoral care with the elderly. Pastors are obviously in a strategic position to respond to developmental needs and life-cycle crises of the aged and their families. In rendering pastoral care pastors also have a unique opportunity to be facilitators and enablers of congregational programs involving the entire community. Unfortunately, pastors sometimes prove to be ill-equipped and uninformed in responding to opportunities for individual and congregational pastoral care with older adults. Their inadequacy appears to be rooted, in part at least, in the pastors' own anxieties and attitudes about the aging process, a problem shared with most people in our society. Pastors are no more likely than anyone else to be comfortable with aging or to be well informed on gerontological issues. While it is impossible to cover all issues in this article, I hope to provide some ideas and resources for pastoral care ministry with older adults. The article is written from the perspective of seeing ourselves as part of the natural process of aging and growing older.

Aging and the Aged: Some Definitions

Aging is a common denominator in human experience and touches all the basic areas of life. Birthdays remind us that we are all aging. Aging begins at conception and runs the full cycle of human life. It is the life-long process of growth and change in which we all

---

[1]David Moberg, "Aging and Theological Education," *Theological Education,* 1980, (Winter), p. 286.

take part. Biblical authors, particularly in the Old Testament, suggest that it is part of God's plan for us that we grow and mature through the successive stages from infancy to old age. The frequent biblical references to aging and old age (for example, some 250 in the Old Testament) suggest the awareness and appreciation of the changing states in the ongoing process of life. Everyone alive is aging.

But when do we become "old" or "elderly"? It is not easy to say when for there is no one set point when we cross middle age to old age. How each of us functions physically and psychologically usually provides a far more helpful description of our aging than the year of our birth. Although defining old age on the basis of organic and behavioral functions may at times be useful and convenient, it is hardly valid or sufficient. Likewise, social roles (for example, when an individual retires, becomes a grandparent, or enters a nursing home), as well as "how old one feels" are sometimes used to define "old," but these, too, are incomplete and inaccurate. In other words, there is no single correct and simple definition or formula for determining when we become "old. " Our definitions seem to vary to suit the person and the occasion. The age of the person responding influences one's definition of "old."

Many demographers, whose job it is to study the composition and patterns of the human population, have recognized the wide diversity in the aging process by dividing those over 55 into four age groups: "older" (55 and over), "elderly" (65 and over), "aged" (75 and over), and "very old" (85 and over). Census statistics, however, still use the one category of age 65 and older to give statistical information about older adults.

The Process of Aging: Continuity and Change

Aging is not one process but many. Any discussion of aging should reflect that it is *a whole person* who is aging and becoming older. This concept of wholeness requires the interfacing of physical, psychological, social, and spiritual dimensions of human growth and development.

Physical changes. Aging is a process that includes *physical changes* in our bodies over the entire life span. In adolescence, our bodies mature, and we become more aware of our sexuality in rather powerful ways. In middle age we are sometimes surprised by our shortness of breath as we rush up two flights of stairs or at discovering a few gray hairs. Our bodies, having moved through periods of maturation and maturity at earlier stages of our lives, gradually lose their capacity for peak performances as we grow older. Sometimes we can't accept that we are getting older. Our high school and college reunions serve to confront us with the reality of the passing of time and the aging process taking place in all of us. Effectiveness in ministry with older adults depends upon our own understanding of and coming to terms with our aging and eventual death. Gerontophobia is very much present in ranks of clergy as well as among medical doctors and others in the health professions.[2]

Decreases and losses related to physical aging come gradually for most of us as we age and do not greatly affect our daily activities. For some of us, however, bodily changes and losses may come more abruptly and harshly alter our general health and lifestyle. It is important and encouraging, therefore, to note that there are often ways to compensate for some of the negative effects of the physical aging process *(e.g.,* hearing aids, advancement in medical treatment and medications, information about nutrition and exercise programs, *etc.).*

Psychological effects. The psychological effects of the passing of time in older adults reveal great variability. Although research suggests that performances closely related to organic functions are negatively influenced by age *(e.g.,* reaction time, recent memory, *etc.),* those based on learning and experience *(e.g.,* vocabulary, problem solving, creativity, *etc.)* are not.[3] In fact, in spite of the more dramatic physical changes and losses that occur, our mental abilities and personalities remain remarkably stable throughout the life span.

Social change. Aging is also a process that includes social change. As we grow older, our roles, relationships, and social and occupational status dynamically shift and change. Retirement, relocation, death of spouse and close friends, and the increase in chronic illnesses challenge us to adapt and adjust to new roles and circumstances.

---

[2]L. Thomas Kucharski, Royce M. White, Jr., and Marjorie Schratz, "Age Bias, Referral for Psychological Assistance and the Private Physician," *Journal of Gerontology,* 1979, Vol. 34, No. 3, pp. 423-428.

[3]Robert Kastenbaum, *Growing Old: Years of Fulfillment* (San Francisco, CA: Harper and Row, 1979), pp. 28-39.

Although aging and becoming an older adult is largely a positive experience for most of us, it is unpredictable and unique for each one of us. In spite of the variety of physical, psychological and social changes that occur as we age, acquired coping skills enable us generally to function with amazing effectiveness. Researchers have demonstrated that as we grow older we develop a valuable reservoir of patterns within which we organize our experience.[4] This allows us to evaluate an experience or crisis and to make decisions about how best to respond. Having experienced some of the sadness and sorrows of life, we have learned something about grieving, adjusting, compensating, and rebuilding. In addition, of course, our life-long experience of God's presence and love in our lives provides us with a sense of trust and hope. Our individual life stories are made up of chapters with events and relationships that have taught us how to face a new day and a new challenge.

Size and Growth of the Older Population

A revolution is underway throughout the world—a global revolution of aging. As evidenced by the increasing number of persons over the age of 65, clearly we have become an aging society. The United States, for example, has since 1800 gradually been changing from a population of youth to a population of adults largely as the result of the elimination of the killer diseases of childhood. In addition, in recent decades the advances in health care and the new medical technology have resulted in more persons living healthier and longer lives. In addition, the lower fertility rates of the last several decades have combined with the decline of mortality rates at older ages to cause a dramatic increase in life expectancy for all of us.

The growth in the number of those who are older is reflected dramatically in the following statistics:

In 1776 only one out of every 50 Americans was over 65. Today one out of nine Americans (11 percent) and one of ten Canadians (10 percent) exceeds 65.

In the last two decades the 65 and older population in the United States has grown twice as fast as the rest of the population.

---

[4]Richard Kalish, *Late Adulthood: Perspectives on Human Development* (Monterey, CA: Brooks/Cole, 1982), 2d ed., pp. 40-42.

By the year 2030 *one* person in *five* will be over 65.

In the year 2050 approximately *one* person in *four* will be over 65.

During the next 50 years the number of persons 75 years and older will more than triple.

By 2050 *one* person in *twelve* in the United States will be at least 80 years old.

Older adults are already a significant and growing group in the church. Most religious denominations in America report that persons over age 65 make up 20 percent or more of their membership.[5] This number is almost twice the percentage of older adults (11 percent) reported overall in our nation's census figures. In most congregations we have only to look around at worship services to observe that many persons are of retirement age and older.

Myths and Misconceptions

Unfortunately, negative images and demeaning stereotypes of older adults still flourish in our society. They project a mental picture of older adults that is exaggerated, negative, inaccurate, prejudicial, and divisive. The portrayal of elderly persons by the media and in advertisements has often perpetuated myths and misconceptions about aging and growing old. Youth is depicted as the best stage of life and old age as the worst. Youth is equated with beauty, strength, vitality and productivity. To be old is equated with being frail, useless, inactive, unattractive and unimportant.

Age stereotyping on television often portrays the older person as cantankerous, senile, dependent, infirm, and generally useless. Organizations like the Gray Panthers[6] have sought to bring pressure to the networks to correct this unfairness and injustice done to those of us who are older and ultimately to all of us by such media images. Because television has the power to shape attitudes and to validate role and status in our society, it has a responsibility to show people at whatever their ages with understanding and sensitivity and not to present caricatures that ridicule and devalue persons. The term "ageism" has been used to describe the stereotyping and discriminating that occur against the old even as "racism" has been used to describe attitudes of discrimination against people of different races.

---

[5]Cedric Tilberg, *Revolution Underway. An Aging Church in an Aging Society* (Philadelphia, PA. Fortress Press, 1984).

We need to challenge the falsehoods and fallacies that perpetuate inaccurate understanding and untruthful information about the realities of aging and growing old.

Aging From a Christian Perspective

Old age is often that stage of life when the battle between integrity and despair is the most intense. Many forces converge to attack the identity and sense of worth of the older person. With the passing years, physical and social changes undermine one's sense of security and wellbeing. It becomes particularly reassuring to remind oneself that the covenant promise made by God with us in our baptism does not end at age 65. God's love is not determined by a person's age or level of productivity but is unconditional and eternal. As Christians our aging can be interpreted from the perspective of God's gracious purpose in our creation and redemption. In our covenant relationship with God we are called to a life larger than our temporal, time-encompassed lives possibly can comprehend. The ministry of Word and Sacrament reminds us daily of God's unconditional acceptance of us as heirs of eternal salvation. Consequently, we need not wonder about time "running out" on us as years unfold and we become older. Aging and dying are natural parts of living, but they are not final. We have been baptized into a faith that outspeaks our death and even our graves! Each of our lives has an eternal destination and meaning.

Even in the midst of suffering that seems to erode many of the past experiences of God's love and goodness, God's covenant promise remains the strong source and foundation of an eternal redeeming love that sustains us at every stage of life and conquers sickness, suffering, and even death. We never outgrow our relationship with God. That unbroken relationship means that our lives have an eternal destination that is not destroyed or defeated by suffering or death. We remind ourselves and each other in the midst of suffering that God has sent his Son so that we may know the eternal depths of his love for us.

The church, the covenant community, provides tremendous resources for us as we age. Here is where the saving grace of our Lord is personalized by the love, caring and service of fellow Christians. In

---

[6] *Gray Panther Media Guide* (Philadelphia, PA: Gray Panthers Media Watch Task Force, 1983).

this caring surrogate family of Christians, the intrinsic dignity and worth of each person regardless of age is affirmed, honored and nourished.

Pastoral Care With The Elderly

The implications for the pastor's ministry with the elderly is obvious from the descriptive overview set forth in the preceding sections. Several foci of the creative and responsible pastoral ministry are deserving of being highlighted:

Pastoral Care as a Generator of Personal and Social Meaning. Is growing old in our society worth one's whole life to attain? That is a crucial question for an elderly person. The challenge of older adulthood is to make sense of life at a stage when losses and changes occur with bewildering and sometimes overwhelming frequency and intensity. James Birren of the Andrus Gerontology Center has reminded the religious sector that its primary purpose is to generate meaning in life.[7] The church, and more especially the pastor in his or her ministry, has an extraordinary and unmatched role for communicating that life at all its stages has meaning and worth. The vitality of a person's life depends upon his or her supply of meanings. As a covenant community of believers, the church has the source and center of the ultimate meaning of life in the proclamation of the gospel. Older persons need a sense of purpose in order to continue to struggle and cope with the eroding and debilitating diminishments that aging and growing old often introduce. In a society that measures life in ways which often devalue and dehumanize, the gospel with its recreative power confronts Christians at whatever stage with a destiny and a purpose. The pastor is the proclaimer of that message in and through pastoral care ministry.

Death The Ultimate Challenge. Facing one's personal death is another of the developmental tasks of old age. Aging with its narrowing boundaries reminds us that we are death-bound creatures. Indeed, to live in time is to live toward death. Dying and death, although not exclusively, are largely thought of as being the business of the elderly. The longer an older person lives, the more members of his

---

[7]James E. Birren, "Gerontology: A Scientific and Value-laden Field of Inquiry," a lecture delivered at Luther Northwestern Seminary, St. Paul, Minnesota, May 4, 1984.

or her family and friends are lost in death. As the final challenge, older persons confront their own dying and death.

Learning how to grieve creatively is essential to learning how to live as well as how to die. Older persons need supportive settings and relationships for dealing with the many grief issues that make up their lives. In addition, in a Christian community an older person should never have to fear dying isolated and alone. Yet that remains the paramount fear of many elderly who have survived their spouses, close friends, and sometimes even their children. While it celebrates a faith that overcomes the grave, the church must strive to be a caring community that comforts those who mourn and attends those who are dying. Traditionally, the pastor has the major role of providing pastoral care to the dying and the bereaved. This ministry demands both skill and faithfulness and must be a priority in the midst of all the demands on the pastor's time.

Life Review as a Method of Pastoral Care and Mutual Ministry. Life review appears to be one of the developmental tasks of the last stage of life. There is a sense of urgency for the elderly to share their life story. One of the developmental tasks of aging is to maintain a past-screening function that reclaims the past. Our personal experiences are always located in time. The fear of forgetting and the need to remember both mark the last stage of life. Memory enables us to hold fast to our identity and to shape and interpret it in new ways. We do not merely have these memories; we are these memories. By remembering we make connections and discover the patterns and design of our lives. Life review provides a configuration, a mosaic of meaning of our lives, and facilitates the next stage which includes death. Life review, in other words, helps older adults tell their story, who they are and where they have been.

Life review, of course, is nothing new. It is normal activity that persons in every culture have engaged in and valued, for reminiscing by way of oral histories has recounted the past and provided cultural wisdom through the ages. Robert Butler, beginning with a seminal article in 1963,[8] introduced reminiscence as a form of life review as a therapeutic tool in the service of ego integrity of older people.

---

[8]Robert Butler, "The Life Review: An Interpretation of Reminiscence in the Aged," *Psychiatry*, 1963, Vol. 24, pp. 65-76.

Butler suggested that life review is a universal experience shared by all older persons, albeit granting different intensities and results:

> Some of the positive results of reviewing one's life can be the righting of old wrongs, making up with enemies, coming to acceptance of mortal life, a sense of serenity and pride in accomplishment, a feeling of having done one's best. It gives people an opportunity to decide what to do with the time left to them and work out emotional and material legacies. People become ready but in no hurry to die.[9]

Recent empirical studies have confirmed the value of life review with older adults. It has proven to help maintain a higher level of functioning, an increase in mental alertness, a greater sense of personal identity, and a reinforcement of coping mechanisms.[10]

The pastoral care implications of life review are obvious and myriad. Memory reveals God's presence in our lives. Faith is the recounting of God's presence and love in our journey through time. Skilled pastoral care that understands the dynamics of life review can help older persons retrieve events from their memories that mediate God's graciousness to them. Furthermore, in the healing word of God's forgiveness that the pastor is able to convey, they escape the sense of despair of old guilts and failures that have continued to fester through time. Because emotional and spiritual options remain open until death, as Butler has reminded us, reconciliation and healing remain viable possibilities.

Life review is a phenomenological approach in seeking to understand the "lived world" of a person. It shifts away from an understanding of pastoral counseling as something that focuses on crisis and is intent on analysis that sometimes becomes reductionistic. Life review is a process that requires responsive listening as a person shares the story of his or her life. It is more than a sentimental journey back through time; it is helping that person identify meanings in his or her life. It means gently nudging persons to reflect on what a joyful or sorrowful event meant in their lives. It chronicles not only a person's encounter with life but with God. It utilizes reminiscence as a pastoral tool for assisting persons in becoming aware of the conti-

---

[9]Robert Butler and Myrna Lewis, *Aging and Mental Health* (St. Louis, MO: C.V. Mosby, 1977), 2d ed., pp. 49-50.

[10]Irene Burnside, *Working with the Elderly* (Monterey, CA: Wadsworth, 1984), 2d ed., pp. 298-307.

nuity and meaning of their lives. The patterns of our lives are shaped by the meaning we give to what we remember.

The skillful use of life review assists pastors in engaging in a ministry that enriches their communication with older adults by validating that "having been" is a valued mode of being. Laity, of course, can be trained to do skillful life review and engage in a mutual ministry of listening and responding that enriches parish visitation programs. Videotapes, such as "A Room Called Remember," are available to introduce basic skills to both pastors and laity.

Gerontological Gender Issues and Pastoral Care. Women comprise the surviving majority in our society. The extension of a woman's life expectancy from approximately 45 years in 1900 to 78.2 years in 1982 represents one of the most revolutionary changes in the twentieth century. A man's life expectancy currently is only 70.9 years.[11] Consequently, in the present "graying of America," women will be culturally defined as *older*—and *Elderly*—for a longer period of time than men. This recent dramatic extension of life expectancy compounds the double jeopardy of ageism and sexism that challenges and confronts older women. Women predominate in the grim statistics of one-person households, reduced income, increased poverty, and greater risk of ill-health, death and institutionalization.[12] For many women widowhood and poverty are always on the horizon.

Demographics by a White House Mini-Conference on Older Women illustrate how the destinies of women are shaped by gender.[13]

> The average age of the onset of widowhood is 56.
>
> 85 percent of surviving spouses are female.
>
> Chances of remarriage for an older women are slim: nine men over 65 remarry for every women who does.
>
> While three-fourths of men in this age group are married, three-fifths of all women 65 and over are unmarried.
>
> Two-thirds of all widows live alone.

---

[11]U.S. Bureau of Census, "America in Transition: An Aging Society," by Cynthia M. Taeubur, Current Population Reports, Special Studies, Series P-23, No. 128 (Washington, DC. U.S. Department of Commerce, 1983).

[12]Elizabeth W. Markson (Ed.), *Older Women. Issues and Prospects* (Lexington, MA: D.C. Health, 1983.)

[13]Statistics presented are from "Facts on Older Women " prepared from the findings of the White House Mini-Conference on Older Women, Des Moines, Iowa, 1980, and from the U.S. Bureau of Census, 1983.

More than one out of every three women 65 and older lives alone, a figure that has doubled in the last 15 years.

Elderly women are twice as likely to be poor as compared to elderly men.

Three-fourths of all nursing home residents are women.

Because of the disproportionally large representation of women who are members of a church and throughout their lifespan maintain a higher church attendance than men, it is mandatory that pastors acquaint themselves with the demographics and issues of aging women and their implications for relevant and innovative pastoral care.[14]

Older women are not a homogeneous population. Although there is a danger of generalizing from the demographic data set forth in the preceding paragraphs and viewing all older women as disadvantaged and even victimized, there is no one pattern of experience of aging for either men or women. If there is one thing characteristic of the elderly population, it is heterogeneity. But there remains an undeniably obvious higher degree of vulnerability for older women in our present society that tragically is deeply ingrained in our present socialcultural-economic system. Questions concerning the meaning of life and suffering, self-definition and worth, sexual and family roles, and attitudes toward care-giving and care-receiving are among the challenging questions that confront older women and those who would render pastoral care to them.[15]

Pastoral Care as Family Surrogate Model. A recent report to the United States House of Representatives Select Committee on Aging (1980) identified the church as a preeminent representative of the voluntary sector that should be encouraged and enabled by the federal government and other concerned groups in our society to assume a more primary role with respect to the elderly. The fact that the church uses a formal/informal family surrogate organizational model, offers multiple educational counseling, and social support programs, and utilizes a mixture of volunteers of all ages, including the current elderly, as well as professional staff, were cited as organizational advantages which are distinct and essential to meeting the needs of an increasing aging population.

---

[14]Barbara Payne, "Religion and the Elderly in Today's World," in Wm. Clements (Ed), *Ministry with the Aging* (San Francisco, CA: Harper and Row, 1981), p. 159.

[15]Melvin A. Kimble, "The Surviving Majority: Differential Impact of Aging and Implications for Ministry," *Word & World*, Vol. 5, No. 4, pp. 395-404.

The theological and biblical resources for ministry and for the expression of the caring community are made visible in the local congregation where the whole family of God is gathered. Here the intrinsic dignity and value of each person regardless of age is affirmed and honored.[16] In such a supportive atmosphere creative pastoral care encourages the sharing of strengths and weaknesses, joy and sorrows, and talents and limitations of all age groups.

In such a ministry, the church follows a historically rich tradition in which the congregation as the household of God becomes the context for loving service to one's neighbor and engages in pastoral care tasks.[17]

Pastoral Care as Advocacy. The church is called to speak the Word of God and to provide a vision of society in which there is justice for the aged. A pastoral care prophetic perspective that introduces a Christian understanding of justice and human rights and that insightfully and responsibly focuses on issues of equity, power, autonomy, and dignity is required if the unique issues and needs of older persons are to be addressed.

The elderly need people willing to stand up for them and with them to seek the necessary changes which will assure them adequate income, housing, food, and health care. In an age-segregated society, the church must be an advocate for the maintenance of programs and policies that will secure benefits to older adults, especially to the elderly poor, the elderly minorities, the homebound, and the isolated. Legal assistance, law enforcement which protects rights and guards safety, supportive services that assist in maintaining independent living, laws that eliminate age discriminatory employment and retirement practices, and nursing home regulations that assure quality care at the end stage of life are but a few of the areas that need to be addressed in pastoral care ministry with the elderly. If the church intends to be an advocate for older adults, it must work both locally and nationally for appropriate legislative action and act as a sentinel in fighting cuts in those programs and services which are beneficial and essential to an older person's wellbeing. Pastors must avoid

---

[16]See my chapter, "Education for Ministry with the Aging," in William Clements (Ed.), *Ministry with the Aging* (San Francisco: Harper and Row, 1981), pp. 209-219.

[17]Jean Laporte, "The Elderly in the Life and Thought of the Early Church," in Wm. Clements (Ed.), *Ministry with the Aging* (San Francisco, CA: Harper and Row, 1981), pp. 37-55.

modeling passivity, indifference, and hopelessness if they are to affirm the contribution of older adults to our society and to secure for them more equal access to its goods and services .

Conclusion

Few roadmaps exist that chart the new pastoral care territories introduced by the increased life expectancy of older adults who for the forseeable future will continue to grow. On the whole, however, future cohorts of the elderly will be healthier, better educated, more politically involved, increasingly active in the work force and in volunteer activities, and generally more assertive and proactive. Because of the large percentage of older adults who are members of the church and participate in congregational life, the pastor has a unique opportunity to share with them in the role of map-maker in the exploration of their new world of longer life expectancy. The pastor can do this by providing creative and responsible pastoral care and supporting the elderly in their quest for wholeness and a human social system that enlarges and enriches their experience of grace and meaning in all stages of their lives, including old age.

Pastoral Care in the Hospital

FRANK S. MOYER, M. A .,
Corporate Consultant on Ethics,
Rockford Memorial Corporation,
2400 N Rockton,
Rockford, IL 61103

I n their 1936 classic, *The Art of Ministering To the Sick,* chaplain Russell L. Dicks and physician Richard C. Cabot asked: *"Has the Protestant minister of today any good reason to visit the sick?* The doctor diagnoses and treats them. The apothecary prepares their medicines. The nurse or the family give bedside care. The social worker looks after domestic, legal and industrial difficulties. The librarian supplies books. The occupational therapist gives manual work. The Catholic priest hears confessions, gives absolution and administers extreme unction. But can the Protestant minister be anything but a nuisance? *By what authority, then, does the minister go to the sick room?"*[1] (emphasis added).

There are even greater challenges to pastoral care in the modern hospital of the late twentieth century! The number of professionals and paraprofessionals involved in the care of the sick have increased significantly, as have the varieties of services offered. Financing these health-care givers and their services has become a national concern that has had a major impact on patients as they struggle with shorter stays and other efforts to control costs. The most dramatic challenge, though, results from changes in our understandings of disease and its genesis and in our expectations for treatment. The knowledge explosion underlying this challenge is the principal factor in the changes evident in the numbers, varieties and costs of services and providers.

Thus patients, health-care givers, hospital administrators and society are engaged today in a highly technical and complex process within which roles, functions, and costs are carefully defined, moni-

---

[1]Richard C. Cabot and Russell L. Dicks, *The Art of Ministering to the Sick* (New York, NY: Macmillan, 1936), p. 3.

tored and contained. It is in the context of that process that we must wrestle with our questions, and our answers will determine whether pastoral care in the hospital is integral, parallel, contradictory or irrelevant to that process.

At an educational program for clergy several years ago, four discharged patients (all of whom were active in their local parishes) and four community clergy (all of whom had many years experience) were asked in separate sessions the question posed by Cabot and Dicks: "Has the Protestant minister of today any good reason to visit the sick?" Their answers were remarkably compatible and identified eight motives, functions or related roles. All of them agreed on "tradition," "friend," "listener," and "witness" as the most important. The laity identified "diversionary" as fifth on their list, while clergy added "membership on the health team," "healer of the estrangement of illness, " and "personal satisfaction" to their list. While two of the functions ("healer" and "team member") openly claim an integral role for the pastor, and none see it as contradictory, the majority would be classified as parallel or irrelevant to the patient-staff-hospital process.

Many voices today cry out for greater integration of pastoral care with those who are sick. Contemporary changes in providing health care have often resulted in a process that is experienced as damaging to patient, staff, and community. Courses and seminars on "Guest Relations," "Wholistic Health Clinics," "Home Health," "Patient Advocacy" and many other topics represent some of the attempts being made to insure a process of caring which is not destructive. Many of these involve clergy and parishes (lay visitation programs, classes on "The Nurse in the Church"). If clergy, parish and health-care givers are to discover ways to integrate programs with pastoral care, then attention must be given to three questions: 1. *By what authority do we visit the sick?* 2. *What is our understanding of disease?* 3. *What objectives do we have in visiting the sick?*

By What Authority Do We Visit the Sick?

Questions—and answers—regarding authority for pastoral care to the sick have existed for centuries. They were apparent in the scriptures (*e.g.* John 9 and the healing of the blind), and their presence throughout history has been ably discussed by John McNeill in

A *History of the Cure of Souls,*[2] by Daniel Williams in *The Minister and the Care of Souls,*[3] among others. As Williams observed: "There is no place in the life of the church where the issues concerning the nature of the minister's authority become more sharply defined or where they lead to more fateful consequences than at the point where he [or she] becomes responsible for a soul in need."[4] While the struggles of modern hospitals, health professionals and clergy with these issues are not substantively different than those experienced throughout history, there are new facets which raise other concerns. Alistair V. Campbell speaks of a confusion "partly caused by the extraordinary successes of the human sciences . . . in shedding light on the causes of human distress and the nature of helping relationships" which helps to alienate us from an emphasis upon "priestly or ministerial authority."[5] What, then, might be some of the sources or images of such an authority?

One source of authority in the care of the sick is *permission.* Has the patient given permission for such care? Certainly the invitation by the sick person to share in his or her journey is important in any assessment of authority. Much has been written about informed consent and the rights of patients. A Presidential Commission stated it quite appropriately: "Informed consent is rooted in the fundamental recognition—reflected in the legal presumption of competency—that adults are entitled to accept or reject health care interventions on the basis of their own personal values and in furtherance of their own personal goals."[6] Determining whether such permission has been given knowingly is, however, not a simple task. Does the patient have all the data? Has the data been presented free from verbal or nonverbal pressures? Is the patient competent to make such a decision? Are the rights of others (*i e.* the hospital staff) also protected by such a decision? At a more pragmatic level, patient confidentiality, scheduling concerns in busy treatment programs and security issues have often resulted in regulations which permit visitors only during

---

[2]John T. McNeill, *A History of the Cure of Souls* (New York, NY: Harper Brothers,1951).

[3]Daniel Day Williams, *The Minister and the Care of Souls* (New York, NY: Harper and Row, 1961).

[4]*Ibid,* p. 30.

[5]Alastair V. Campbell, *Rediscovering Pastoral Care* (Philadelphia, PA: Westminster 1981), p 13.

[6]President's Commission for the Study of Ethical Problems in Medicine and Biomedical and Behavioral Research, *Making Health Care Decisions; A Report on the*

identified times. Thus, *permission* alone is a limited source of authority for the pastor who seeks to visit the sick.

A second source for authority, given considerable attention in recent decades, is *knowledge*. Historically, parishioners and others have recognized clergy as being among the educated in their midst, but the concern with knowledge has been given a new impetus in the proliferation of specialties in the various helping professions. Credentials have become critical as a wary public hopes to identify qualified helpers.

Much recent effort in pastoral care education has focused upon the development of an expertise which can be identified and certified. Clergy have participated in Clinical Pastoral Education programs, in organizations such as the Academy of Parish Clergy and in the various professional certification processes offered by the Association for Clinical Pastoral Education, College of Chaplains, Association of Mental Health Clergy, National Association of Catholic Chaplains, and others. As with other professionals, authority for the pastoral visit would be founded upon education, certification, and peer review.

While the *knowledge* level concerning the human sciences among clergy has been demonstrably strengthened, it has proved to be of limited value as a source of authority for pastoral care of the sick. Theological consensus in our society does not exist, nor is it particularly desired! As Campbell observed, "However much some theologians and church leaders might wish it otherwise, the absence of doctrinal unanimity—and the *welcoming* of this—remains a feature of our time."[7] Nor is there consensus among the other human sciences, as indicated by a statement of Carl Rogers' which Campbell cites: "It has gradually been driven home to me that I cannot be of help . . . by means of any intellectual or training procedure. No approach which relies upon knowledge, upon training, upon the acceptance of something that is *taught,* is of any use . . . The failure of any such ap-

Ethical and Legal Implications of Informed Consent in the Patient Practitioner Relationship, Vol. 1 (Washington, DC: U.S. Government Printing, Office, 1982).
   [7]Campbell, *Rediscovering Pastoral Care,* p. 16.

proach through the intellect has forced me to recognize that change appears to come about through experience in a relationship."[8]

For others today, experience in a relationship has become the source of their authority for pastoral care of the sick. The church has always had a strong interest in the ministry of all believers, and there are many today who are quite willing to implement such ministries. Since there is little agreement on *knowledge,* relationship seems to be all the authority needed. That source appears primarily informed by a personal relationship between the care giver and his or her God and of their understanding of how such an experience might be helpful to the patient. They come in a spirit of friendship—and trust that the visit will be beneficent.

Certainly the value of friendship as a major pastoral resource is significant. In *The Christian Pastor,* Wayne E. Oates identifies it as the first level of pastoral care. "The ministry of friendship is the indispensable necessity for all other deeper levels of pastoral work. It is the seedbed of any fruitful service to people. Furthermore, a great majority of the real help that comes to people in crises is through persons whom they would term 'just a good friend' and not through professional people."[9] However, friendship is neither the authority upon which our visits are founded nor the objective of those visits. Many persons offer friendship to those who are sick, and do so successfully, independent from professional education for, or ordination to, ministry! Also, as Oates further states, "the most outstanding limitation of the social level of a pastor's ministry [is that] there are some things a person can tell only to a stranger."[10]

The shortcomings of *permission, knowledge* and *relationship* as sufficient sources of authority are illustrated in an incident reported several years ago. A parish in England employed a man who was a skilled public speaker to preach and conduct worship, but who was also an avowed atheist! He certainly had permission and expertise, and his willingness to associate with a parish was indicative of a "faith" relationship. Yet few would argue that such a ministry had *au-*

---

[8]*Ibid.,* pp. 21-22. The statement appears originally in Rogers' essay, ''Some Hypotheses Regarding the Facilitation of Personal Growth," in *On Becoming a Person* (Boston, MA: Houghton Mifflin, 1961), pp. 32ff.

[9]Wayne E. Oates, *The Christian Pastor* (Philadelphia, PA: Westminster, 1964), p. 162.

[10]*Ibid* ., p. 164.

thority. Even though he was hired to perform some of the tasks of ministry, there was no Call or sense of vocation to give his work authority.

Cabot and Dicks answered the issue of authority in these words: "The minister goes to the sickroom because he is the duly recognized representative of Him. "[11] Joseph Sittler, in *Gravity and Grace,* defines pastoral authority in terms which include Word and Sacrament: "The Church insists on preparing a designated cadre to see to it that the constitutive story is told, and that the nurturing sacraments are administered."[12] Pastoral care of the sick confronts you in multiple ways with your Call. When you visit the sick *as a pastor,* you enter that person's pain. That, in itself, demands something unique of you as a person, and it is to this that Henri Nouwen refers when he remarks, in his book *In Memoriam,* that "I realized that sorrow is an unwelcome companion and that anyone who willingly enters into the pain of a stranger is truly a remarkable person."[13]

Entering into another's pain also demands something unique in your understanding of other persons and of care. Tillich speaks to this in his essay on "Theology of Pastoral Care":

> When I hear the term *pastoral care,* I sometimes imagine myself to be in the situation of receiving pastoral care, and imagining this, I somehow feel humiliated. Someone else makes me an object of his care, but no one wants to become an object and, therefore, he resists such situations like pastoral care . . . There are two reasons for this possibility. The first is the fact that care, including pastoral care, is something universally human. It is going on always in every moment of human existence. The second more important reason is that care is essentially mutual: [the one] who gives care also receives care.[14]

Failure to recognize this important uniqueness is damaging to the patient because it perpetuates a passive stance in the healing process. Michael Wilson puts it quite beautifully: ". . . as we approach this sick [person, she or he] speaks to us in a voice we do not recognize. 'It is I . . . Inasmuch as ye did it unto one of these my children, .

---

[11]Cabot and Dicks, *The Art of Ministering to the Sick,* p. 12.

[12]Joseph Sittler, *Gravity and Grace* (Minneapolis, MN: Augsburg, 1986), p. 52.

[13]Henri J.M. Nouwen, *In Memoriam* (South Bend, IN: Ave Maria Press, 1980), p. 14.

[14]Paul Tillich, "The Theology of Pastoral Care," in *Clinical Education for the Pastoral Ministry,* ed. the Advisory Committee on Clinical Pastoral Education, 1958, pp. 1-6.

. . ye did it unto me.' (Matthew 25:40)."[15] Failure in this matter also results in damage to the pastor, which James M. Gustafson refers to as becoming a "pseudo-charismatic manipulator."[16]

Your authority arises from your Call and all that has been associated with your process in discerning it, preparing for it, and affirming it. Your *permission, knowledge* and *relationship* are completely intertwined with your understanding of that Call. In *Prophetic Imagination,* Walter Brueggemann suggests some implications of that Call which are helpful to remember as you go to visit the sick. Using the story of Moses leading the Israelites from Egypt, Brueggemann sees the need for a pastoral care enhanced by a prophetic imagination, an imagination that posits a free God, not bound by any system or culture. "If we believe in a free God—free to come and go, free from and even against the regime, free to hear and even answer slaves cries, free from all proper godness as defined by the empire—then [our belief, our faith] will impact life and make justice and compassion possible."[17]

Pastoral care of the sick, in and out of the hospital, must always be defined in terms of the authority of the Call. Tillich's argument that care is both universal and mutual reminds us that there are many giving care in God's name, and that the forms of the giving are not easily distinguishable by the title of the one caring. In short, we have no monopoly on either care or any particular form. Our authority is the Call and the process we use daily to discern continually that call. If you believe that God has called you to visit the sick, as God called Moses, Jonah, Mary, Mary Magdalene, Paul, Hildegard of Bingen and countless other men and women in history, then you have the responsibility to wrestle with the purposes for that visit— "sustaining, healing, guiding, reconciling."[18] Only in that context will theological superficiality and psychological manipulation in our visits be avoided!

The wise pastor regularly takes time to reflect upon the authority which serves as the foundation for his or her visits to the sick.

---

[15]Michael Wilson, "Violence and Nonviolence in the Cure of Disease and the Healing of Patients," *The Christian Century,* 1970, (June 17), p. 757.

[16]*Clinical Education for the Pastoral Ministry, p.* 7.

[17]Walter Brueggemann, *Prophetic Imagination* (Philadelphia, PA: Fortress, 1978).

[18]Don S. Browning, *The Moral Context of Pastoral Care* (Philadelphia, PA: Westminster, 1976).

Those visits are sacred opportunities for proclaiming the ancient and living message of God's journey with the infirm and suffering. God's claim on your life, represented in your Call, is your authority. It is an awesome task and deserves your fullest attention.

What Is Our Understanding of Disease?

And the Lord will take away from thee all sickness, and will put none of the evil diseases of Egypt, which thou knowest, upon thee; but will lay them upon all them that hate thee. [Deuteronomy 7:15 KJV]

And, behold, there came a leper and worshipped him, saying, Lord, if thou wilt, thou canst make me clean. [Matthew 8:2 KJV]

Is any sick among you? Let him call for the elders of the church; and let them pray over him, anointing him with oil in the name of the Lord: And the prayer of faith shall save thc sick, and the Lord shall raise him up; and if he have committed sins, they shall be forgiven him. [James 5:14-15 KJV]

Throughout much of recorded history, men and women believed that disease was caused by God, or by evil spirits working upon or through a person's body or by styles of patterns of behavior which, in themselves, were either evil or in dissonance with the mores of the society. Diagnosis meant an examination of a person's relationship with the Divine, with the community, and with ones own self. Certainly the spiritual director or advisor played an important role in the life of the sick person.

Unfortunately, such an approach often hindered the advances of scientists as they sought to gain better understandings of the pathophysiology of disease and frequently burdened the sick with isolation and judgment. Disease is now believed to be caused by chemical agents, bacteria, viruses, genes, and anatomical malformations. Certain lifestyles are still to be avoided, but for reasons of health rather than any communal morality. As modern technological medicine exploded with knowledge, the doctor replaced the shaman, the medicine man or woman, the witch doctor, and the priest or priestess. If today's pastoral-care giver identifies closely with the historical view of disease, she or he will find minimal acceptance from parishioners and even less from hospital staff and personnel. Yet close identification with the modern view frequently results in a pastoral ministry which focuses on supportive factors associated with the patient's attitude toward the disease. At best this is a process parallel to the work of modern medicine and contributes little to either an understanding of the origin of the disease or its actual treatment.

Nor are pastors the only persons troubled with these contrasting views of disease. Harold Merskey, Professor of Psychiatry at London Psychiatric Hospital, London, Ontario, writes:

> It is argued that there is no agreed definition of disease. Purely biological definitions are inadequate and combined biological and social definitions are not yet satisfactory . . . In practice, the weight given to the idea of disease varies according to what it will imply about obligations and privileges.[19]

Noted bioethicist H. Tristram Engelhardt, Jr., observes that

> physicians have come to use the word disease to designate the underlying nexus of causal forces that produces the symptoms experienced by the patient, which cluster of symptoms is often referred to as an illness. There is a temptation, then, to think of this underlying structure as discoverable without reference to particular values.[20]

And in *The Healer's Art,* Eric J. Cassell uses these most poetic words in describing our confusion over the meaning of disease:

> The drama of medical care is carried out in the arena of society; and while the primary roles are played by patient and doctor, other members of the social group play active roles. In our culture the rules for this interplay seem to have been stable for a long time, but today the rules are changing because of the technological revolution of our times . . . The success of medicine has created a strain: the doctor sees his role as the curer of disease and "forgets" his role as healer of the sick; and, patients wander disabled but without a culturally acceptable mantle of disease with which to clothe the nakedness of their pain.[21]

The sick in our age need a definition of disease which will bring their "whole" self into clear focus and avoid any fragmentation into a mind-body-soul division. Such a definition has been offered by chaplain Robert Reeves in his classic article (and cassette tape), "The

---

[19]Harold Merskey, "Variable Meanings for the Definition of Disease," *Journal of Medicine and Philosophy,* 1986, Vol. 11, pp. 215-32.

[20]H. Tristram Englehardt, Jr., "Clinical Complaints and the *Ens Morbi,*" *Journal of Medicine and Philosophy,* 1986, Vol. 11, pp. 207-14.

[21]Eric J. Cassell, *The Healer's Art* (Cambridge, MA: MIT Press), pp. 50-51.

Meaning and Message of Illness": *Disease is the response of the organism as a whole to whatever seriously alters its equilibrium.*[22]

Let us examine certain aspects of Reeves' definition. First, disease is a response. Much of our common language speaks of disease as if it is something that happens to us: "The flu bug got me," or "I had a heart attack," or "I don't know why this happened to me." Such language reflects the belief that the sick individual is relieved of responsibility for his or her illness. She or he is a victim, and cannot be held liable for what has happened. That concept has produced many positive results. Developments such as sick pay benefits and the availability of treatment programs for substance abuse are but two of these. Society is certainly served when individuals and families are not destroyed financially and when assistance is substituted for judgment.

The price for the patient, however, is a sense of victimization in a secular medical world which no longer gives significant credence to the presence of evil as a reality. If medicine did so believe, such a concept would at least open the person to the realm of his or her psyche and soul. Treatment would require behavior changes directed at appeasing the gods or vanquishing evil. Modern health care, despite recent commentary by such people as Scott Peck in *People of the Lie* or Karl Menninger in *Whatever Became of Sin?* is essentially devoid of any consideration of the lie, the sin or the evil. Reeves' definition highlights an awareness that disease is a response. That is, disease is a person's answer or reply, behaviorally, and treatment must not only focus upon that reply, but must also discover the question (or stimulation).

The second aspect of Reeves' definition which deserves our attention is that the response is of *the organism as a whole.* Hospitals and health care organizations generally strive to design their programs so as to offer treatment to "whole persons." These can range from well-staffed Pastoral Services, Social Services and Guest Relation programs to HBO, art carts and landscaping. Each of these has supportive research literature indicating its contribution to getting well quicker or staying well longer. While many of these services struggle with decreasing finances, modern marketing concerns dictate their

---

[22]Robert Reeves, "What Makes the Critter Tick?" *Care Cassettes,* Vol. 1, No. 1. The College of Chaplains, 1974.

continued presence in some form. Yet almost all of these are viewed as ancillary services and are seldom used diagnostically. Reeves would insist, however, that persons might experience disease as a response to such stimuli as value conflicts, family stress, and even aesthesia.

An approach which does not see the whole as significant in the genesis of a disease is, at best, one which seeks only to remove symptoms. The bug is destroyed, the heart muscle is repaired, the "bad" organ is removed, and the patient returns home without struggling with the meaning of the disease—"Why are you sick, now?" More than a century ago the medical researcher Claude Bernard said: "Illnesses hover constantly about us, their seeds blown by the wind, but they do not set in the terrain unless the terrain is ready to receive them."[23] And Louis Pasteur is reported to have acknowledged in his final words: "Bernard is right. The germ is nothing; the terrain all."[24]

Reeves' final phrase also merits attention. "Disease is a response of the organism as a whole to whatever seriously alters its equilibrium." First, the "whatever" recognizes stimuli beyond the narrow limits of the physical or physiological. Technology may hear a patient's symptoms and respond that all tests indicate there is nothing wrong. Allowing for "whatever" helps assure that the patient will not be abandoned. Second, the word "equilibrium" introduces the concept of homeostasis. Living organisms seek to achieve balance in order to insure survival. A sliver under the skin is slowly forced to the surface through mechanisms which could be viewed as symptoms of a disease. So too with many other adaptations to the stresses of everyday life. Hans Selye's work on stress indicates that each person has a general adaptive syndrome which, if stressed enough, can adapt to the point of sickness.[25] (Radiation oncologist 0. Carl Simonton lifts this up for his patients when he asks: "Why do you think you have cancer at this time?")[26]

---

[23]Lawrence LeShan, *The Mechanic and the Gardener* (New York, NY: Holt, Rinchart and Winston, 982), p. 57.

[24]*Ibid.*

[25]Hans Selye, *The Stress Of Life* (Toronto: McGraw-Hill, 1956).

[26]0. Carl Simonton, Stephanie Matthews-Simonton, and James L. Creighton, *On Getting Well Again* (New York, NY: Bantam Books, 1980).

If we believe that the whole of a person involves a dynamic integration of spirit-mind-body-community, then disease would be related to that dynamic. Furthermore, we would affirm to the patient that many of the symptoms which are experienced as unwelcome are, in fact, communications from the whole which suggest areas or concerns which need attention. Such an affirmation eliminates the notion of a victim and invites the patient into a partnership with his or her healers.

If we are to overcome the dualism in both the understanding of disease and treatment resources which fragments patients, then pastors must involve themselves in the struggle to define disease more wholistically. The work of Reeves is but one suggestion. Today there are many voices insisting that such a paradigm for disease is needed. Lawrence LeShan, the Simontons, Eric Cassell, Norman Cousins, and others call us to change our concept to one that is more (w)holistic.[27]

What Are Our Objectives in Visiting Sick?

In *The Art of Ministering to the Sick,* Cabot and Dicks stated three goals or objectives of the pastoral visit.[28] While recognizing the changes since 1936, those divisions are still useful:

a) *To counteract the evils of specialization.* One may only speculate at the reaction of the authors to today's scene of specialists, sub-specialists and super-sub-specialists! The exponential growth of knowledge relative to the parts and workings of human life is both the cause and the result of an increase in specialization. Hopefully they would be grateful for a development which has enabled medicine to offer hope far beyond the dreams of our fathers and mothers.

In itself, specialization is not an evil, nor are those who pursue it to be condemned. Rather, it is the misuse or abuse of specialization which is the source of the evils we need to counteract. These evils include a fragmentation of the individual which treats him or her as little more than one body part; the pursuit of knowledge with little concern for the value or cost to the patient and to society; the loss of a generalist advocate who is able to assist the patient in her or his journey through the maze of specialties and institutional regulations

---

[27]Norman Cousins, *Anatomy of an Illness* (New York, NY: Norton, 1979).
[28]Cabot and Dicks, *The Art of Ministering to the Sick,* p. 3.

and the isolation from the healing community of family and friends which occurs as the many specialist helpers become a barrier to such interaction. The presence of each of these is well documented in the literature. So too are the many outcries against it.

The caring pastor counteracts such evils in at least two ways: *first,* by recognizing that such evil exists and is a theological issue. The misuse and abuse of specialization occurs when individuals operate from a value system which is faulty or ineffective in the face of philosophical questions concerning the nature, beginning and end point of life and issues related to the uses of technology, and knowledge and limited resources. These value systems are faulty due to a belief system which functions as if knowledge, science or technology is God and are ineffective due to an educational process which has not assisted values clarification. Pastors may address such issues as Preacher, as Priest, as Teacher, and as Administrator. There is no other professional in our society with such unique opportunities. *Second,* a pastor may counteract the evils arising from specialization in a very specific manner by serving as his or her parishioner's advocate in relating to the health system. This requires a ministry which does not attempt to smooth over problems resulting from abuses or misuses of specialization and treatment. It demands a ministry that is unwilling to function only parallel to the health team, and which is willing to move assertively into relationships wherein data and evaluations and prognoses are shared. Such a ministry will probably not endear the pastor to the persons within that health care system and may result in the loss of some privileges and perquisites of office (clergy parking, relaxed visiting hours, notification of patient admission and the like). However, the value of such a pastor will greatly exceed any loss of either stature or privilege.

b) *To give a devotion such as only religion can permanently inspire.* A familiar story tells of a rich person observing a nun cleansing excrement from a dying patient and saying, "I wouldn't do that for a million dollars," to which the nun replies, "Nor would I." Such devotion is what pastors ought to bring to patients. Cabot and Dicks remarked that "devotion is the minister's badge of office when he [or she] goes to a sufferer." It is also an answer to the question, "By what right do I visit this sick person?"—"only by right of serving you."[29]

---

[29] *Ibid.,* p. 12.

In practical terms, this will require greater preparation by the pastor before the visit, including reviewing what is known about the patient's spiritual development, personal and family history and work relationships; creatively imagining what might be issues and concerns in both the causes and the results of his or her illness and hospitalization and seeking out knowledge about the particular disease process from physicians, nurses, chaplains and others in order to better gain a wholistic picture. Finally, the pastor must commit himself or herself in meditation and prayer to offer personal availability to the patient both in the hospital as well as during recuperation at home.

Such devotion also requires an investment of time after each visit. Pastors need to develop their own charting or note systems, rather than arrogantly acting as if their memories were sufficient. We need to further seek out the other care givers—physicians, nurses, chaplains, social workers, family members—and share and critique our assessments. And we need to spend a few moments in planning for and about our future ministries with each patient. Such devotion is represented in the statement of Jesus that "I was sick and ye visited me." It is costly in terms of time and energy, yet it is the greatest gift the pastor offers to the patient, the patient's family and the other care-givers.

c) To care for the growth of souls. Cabot and Dicks raised three questions which pastors must consider in caring for the growth of souls: "Is all growth spiritual growth?" "What are the foods of growth?" and "Why is one [individual's] growth-food another's poison?"[30] Discovering answers in order to minister effectively is a significant challenge. Spiritual growth occurs best when the assistance given meets the individual's growing edges. Pastors, as well as others, frequently assume in offering help that the person is much further along in the process of spiritual growth. "Have faith," "pray," "trust in God," are too often used in a way that stops or interferes with the process. The crisis of disease and illness strips away the bland platitudes symptomatic of spiritual stagnation and opens the person to both the dangers and the opportunities involved in exploring new spiritual growth. This is not an easy task for the pastor. It requires time for truly understanding what and where the patient is and patience with that location. And what is perhaps even more difficult, it

---

[30] *Ibid.*, p. 13.

demands the pastor's willingness to grow also. The mutuality of care referred to earlier includes a mutuality of spiritual growth. As pastors wrestle with questions of suffering, their theologies will either grow or wither.

The "food" or matrix needed for spiritual growth may be offered in varieties of ways, yet will usually represent one or more of the five categories suggested by Cabot and Dicks: "love, learn[ing], beauty, service and suffering well borne."[31] Each of these is worthy of dedicated time for reflection and consideration in the pastor's own spiritual development, as well as in his or her ministries with the sick.

Love is essential for growth—all growth. Love is gentle as well as hard; encouraging as well as challenging; fulfilling as well as demanding. Loving your patient will not always be easy! Persons who are sick can be demanding, insensitive and uncaring. While our task is not to judge, neither is it to confront the ill with bland superficialities or passive-aggressive infrequencies of visitation. Loving the patient will engage the pastor in a dynamic strong enough to stand against those elements in modern health care which can be violently damaging to a person's well-being.

To *learn is* to recognize the teaching opportunity of disease and illness. Disease is an opportunity for learning, and the wise pastor offers himself or herself as a mentor, raising questions which encourage self-reflection and awareness and providing or seeking information about the body and about the disease. In the face of a slow and tedious challenge, the pastor will give encouragement.

Beauty is vital to healing. One recent study observed shorter hospital stays for surgical patients whose windows offered views of trees![32] Even in 1936 Cabot and Dicks noted the need for an appreciation of beauty in this country. While we may not be able to insure windows which look out to trees, we can work to insure art work suitable to the particular struggle of a particular patient, to develop state-of-the-art interior decorating that is stress-reductive for both patients and staff and to encourage the uses of audio and visual media that lift a patient's horizons beyond the sterility and despair which do exist in hospitals. We certainly can do this in the way we offer our patients the sacraments while hospitalized. Well-designed commu-

---

[31] *Ibid.*, p. 16.

nion and baptismal wares, linens, candles, flowers—these would add considerably to enhancing beauty in the patient's life. Beauty would also include the good use of humor. Cabot and Dicks knew this almost 50 years before Norman Cousins called our attention to it in *Anatomy of an Illness.* While this is not an open invitation to make the pastoral visit a string of jokes, it is a reminder that humor does offer a healthy means of detachment from situations which threaten to engulf us.

Service as a means for spiritual growth refers to our attitude toward the patient's worth as an individual. Rehabilitation centers require this by demanding that patients learn to feed, dress and move themselves to the limits of their capabilities. Cardiac and oncology units challenge patients to discover ways to live fully with their diseases, rather than surrender meekly as if they had no value in life. Pastors ought to do no less. Patients may also be members of prayer chains for others. Recuperating patients may be invited to share their stories with others in order to broaden the teaching value. Shut-ins may be asked to make telephone calls, fold bulletins or stuff envelopes. Each human being, but especially each patient, needs to have affirmed that he or she is still of service to the community.

Suffering well borne, while appropriate as food for growth, is easier to see retrospectively than prospectively. Certainly there are dangers in even mentioning it. It should never be used as a dictum to the patient to stifle expressions of pain, anger and guilt. No circle in hell is too low for those who would use it in such a manner. Rather, it is most useful as a tenet or belief from which the pastor can operate. It is a truth which encourages him or her when the journey with the sufferer becomes long and discouraging—a reminder that growth is essentially a process and not a goal.

Pastoral care in the modern hospital has become exceedingly complex. Such ministry challenges our vocation, stretches our understanding of what it means to be sick, and demands an attention to and struggle with our theologies. It requires us to become knowledgeable of human dynamics, including the processes of disease, and to be creative in our applications and forms of ministry. Further,

---

[32]R.S. Ulrich, "View Through Window May Influence Recovery from Surgery," *Science,* 1984, Vol. 224, pp. 420-421.

it must usually be done in a hierarchical, interdisciplinary system in which the pastor has, at best, an ill-defined role and acceptance.

Involvement in another's struggle with disease is a rare and a demanding privilege. "I was sick and ye visited me" is a helpful paradigm for that involvement and the source of grace for an involvement which is so often beyond our skills.

Index

abuse, 2, 17
Academy of Parish Clergy, 100
Aging and Mental Health (Butler
  & Lewis), 91
Ahlskog, Gary R., 15
Aist, Clark S., 35
Alanon, 22
Alanteen, 22
Alcoholics Anonymous, 22
alcoholism, 24, 46
Allport, Gordon W., 56
American Association of
  Pastoral Counselors, 24, 31
American Journal of Psychiatry, 17
American Psychiatric
  Association, 17, 44
*Americans View Their Mental
  Health* (Gurin), 35
AMHC Forum, 50
Anatomy of an Illness (Cousins),
  108, 112
Andrus Gerontology Center, 89
Art of Ministering to the Sick, The
  (Cabot & Dicks), 97, 108
Association for Clinical Pastoral
  Education, The, 24, 31, 80,
  100
Association of Mental Health
  Clergy, 100
Australian Council of
  Churches, 65
Avery, William 0., 74

Barth, Karl, 73
Basic Types of Pastoral Counseling
  (Clinebell), 72
Bernard, Claude, 107
Bible (reference to), 19, 23, 24,
  26, 33, 45, 65, 70, 72, 73, 74,
  81, 84, 103, 104
Bingen, 103
Birren, James E., 89
Brister, C. W., 72, 73
Browning, Don S., 103
Brueggemann, Walter, 103
Burns, Robert, 79
Burnside, Irene, 91
Butler, Robert, 90, 91

Cabot, Richard C., 97, 98, 102,
  108, 109, 110, 111, 112
Campbell, Alastair V., 99, 100
Can-surmount, 22
Capps, Donald E., 39
Care Cassetts, 106
Cassell, Eric J., 105, 108
Christian Century, The, 103
Christian Pastor, The (Oates),
  70, 101
Christianity, 36, 51, 57, 88, 89,
  94, 103
Church, 35, 40-42, 45, 48, 49,
  53, 65, 66, 67, 70, 71, 72, 87,
  88, 89, 93, 94, 99, 101
Church Dogmatics (Barth), 73
Clebsch, William A., 73, 76
Clements, William, 93, 94
Clinebell, Howard J., 72